ICELAND

The Dorothy Dunnett Guide

Alyson JK Bailes

THE DOROTHY DUNNETT SOCIETY
Edinburgh

dorothydunnett.org

In memory of Dorothy Dunnett, who gave so much pleasure to so many.

There is no land uninhabitable or sea unnavigable.
(The Ringed Castle, *part 3, chapter 9)*

Contents

Maps

Introduction

Iceland is the scene of action in only one of Dorothy Dunnett's works, *To Lie With Lions*, the sixth volume in the House of Niccolò series. In *To Lie With Lions*, a journey made to Iceland in March 1472 by the central character, Nicholas de Fleury – at this stage based in Scotland – forms an extended episode mid-way through the book. Nicholas sails in his new ship *Svipa* (Icelandic 'whip') to try to corner the early season's supply of stockfish, a traditional food made from gutted, wind-dried cod and valued for its long-keeping qualities. He takes with him his Scottish squire Robin of Berecrofts and is joined on the way by Katelijne (Kathi) Sersanders, niece of Anselm Adorne. On first arrival at the Westmann Isles off Iceland's south-west coast, the *Svipa* outsmarts both the *Pruss Maiden,* a German (Hanseatic) ship commanded by Paúel Benecke of Danzig, and another vessel, the *Unicorn*, manned by Nicholas's commercial rivals the Vatachino, which happens to be carrying Kathi's brother Anselm Sersanders. Nicholas gets the stockfish, but the Vatachino vessel manages to slip away and loads a profitable cargo of sulphur at Hafnarfjörður on the west coast.

In tracking Anselm and Kathi, who try to escape overland, Nicholas and Benecke (now his prisoner) end up visiting the episcopal residence of Skálholt, and are drawn further inland while first following the track of a polar bear and then visiting the hot springs at Geysir. From there they see eruptions starting both in the nearby volcano Hekla and under the ice-cap of Katla. Anselm, injured, is left behind but the others – with their Icelandic guide Glímu-Sveinn – attempt a desperate trek across the southern Icelandic interior to rejoin Robin and the *Svipa* at the Markarfljót river estuary.[1] They make it just

PLACE-NAMES AND PRONUNCIATION

Icelandic words are always pronounced as written but the rules of pronunciation are very different from English. The following rough guide may help:

First, the extra letters in the Icelandic alphabet:

ð/Ð is like th in *thick*
þ/Þ is like th in *this*
æ/Æ is like *eye*
ö/Ö is like the French sound in *deux*, or like a shortened u in *fur*
(NB, in a dictionary or gazetteer, *ð* comes after *d* and the other three letters come at the end after *z*)

Throughout *To Lie With Lions*, as is normal in English, Dorothy Dunnett has substituted *Th* for *Þ* and *d* for *ð*. For example, Thjórsá, Thrihyrningur and Hlídarendi for Þjórsá, Þrihyrningur and Hlíðarendi.

Other special pronunciations, including the effect of accents:

á is like *Ow!*
au is like French *oeuil*
é is like a short version of *yea* (and includes the *y* sound)
ei is like the vowel in *hey*
i is short as in *bit*
í is long as in *beet*
f between vowels is similar to *v*; before l, n and t it is similar to *b* or *p*, thus Höfn sounds like Hö*p*n, Keflavik like Ke*b*lavik
g between vowels is very soft, almost a *y* sound (thus vegur = *veyr*)
hr at the start of a word is like *khr* (with *kh* sounding like *ch* in *loch*)
j is always pronounced like *y* in *you*
ll is pronounced roughly like *tl* or *dl*
ó is somewhere between the vowels in *owl* and *bowl*
ú is like *oo*
y and ý are always vowels and are pronounced the same as Icelandic i and í

Sample (approximate) pronunciations of main place names. The first syllable is always stressed, and any subsequent stresses are shown with underlining:

Bessastaðir = Bessa-<u>stath</u>-eer (soft *th*)
Dyrhólaey = Deer-<u>hole</u>-ah-eh
Eyjafjallajökull (the volcano that erupted and brought air traffic to a halt in 2010) = Eh-ya-<u>fyat</u>-la-<u>yuk</u>-utl
Fljótshólar = Flyohts–<u>hole</u>-ar
Flúðir = Floo-theer (soft *th*)
Geysir = Gay-sseer
Gullfoss = Gudl-fohss
Hafnarfjörður = Hapna-<u>fjur</u>t-thuh (soft *th*)
Hlíðarendi = Khlee-thar-<u>end</u>ee (soft *th*)
Hvítá = Khveet-ow
Hvolsvöllur = Khvolls-<u>vutl</u>-uh
Landeyjarhöfn = Land–eh–ya-<u>hupn</u>
Markarfljót = Marr-karr-<u>flyoht</u>
Skálholt = Scowl-holt
Skarð = Scart-th (soft *th*)
Vestmannaeyjar = Vestman-na-<u>eh</u>-yar
Þjórsá = Thyohr-sow

in time but witness the awesome spectacle of Katla in full blast, a disaster that will cause huge suffering for the Icelandic people.

Iceland also provides an essential backdrop to Dorothy Dunnett's free-standing novel *King Hereafter*, based on the thesis that Earl Thorfinn the Mighty of Orkney was one and the same with King Macbeth of Scotland. Two Icelandic characters have significant parts in *King Hereafter*'s plot – Bishop Ísleifr and Arnór the Earls' Poet – and references from Icelandic literature and mythology embody the Norse cultural tradition that competes with Celtic and Christian influences for Thorfinn's allegiance.

This guide aims to help and inform readers of Dorothy Dunnett who are interested in following some or all of Nicholas's route in Iceland, while learning more of the local background. The central part of the text provides an itinerary that tracks Nicholas's journey on land, suggesting routes as near as possible to the original that can be followed by car.

Please note that this guide cannot replace either a good driving map or a general-purpose tourist guidebook. You can buy or order good guides in many world languages before coming to Iceland, but the best maps may only be available in Icelandic bookshops (less often in filling stations) after your arrival. A wealth of material also exists online, and some key websites are listed at the end of this guide.

PLANNING YOUR VISIT

Most travellers to Iceland will start their visit in the capital, Reykjavík, after flying in to Keflavík international airport 50 km west of the city (where cars can be hired). A few, wishing to bring their own vehicles, use the Smyril Line's Norræna summer ferry service from northern Denmark and arrive at Seydísfjörður, two full days' drive to the north-east. In this guide it is assumed that Reykjavík will be your starting-point, and you should indeed plan to spend one to two days there to visit nearby sites named in *To Lie With Lions* (see p. 40) and several good museums.

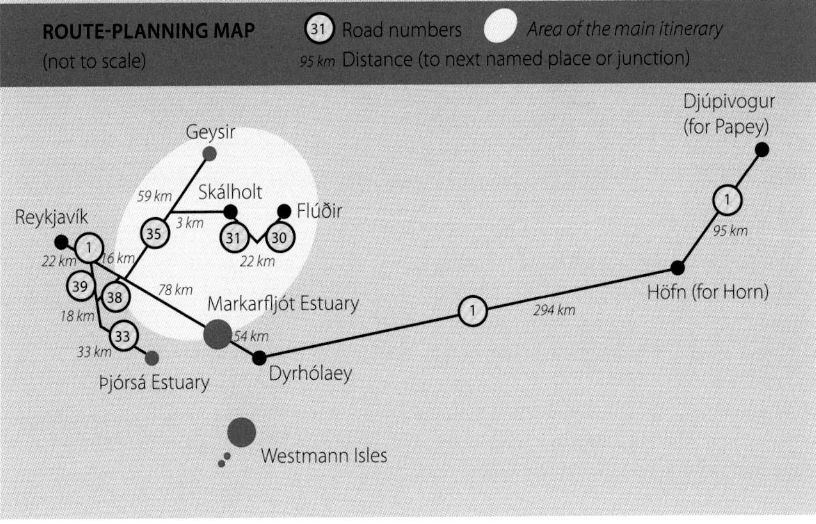

The Land Itinerary

The route travelled by Nicholas and his companions makes a large clockwise loop through south-west Iceland, starting at the mouth of the Þjórsá river south-east of Reykjavík, and returning to the coast further east at the Markarfljót river estuary, opposite the Westmann Isles. This is the area covered in detail in the main section below, which starts by guiding you from Reykjavík to the Þjórsá estuary. That is a drive of around 90 km, and the rest of the itinerary to Markarfljót covers some 380 km by car. (The length is magnified because the modern road system diverges greatly from a 15th-century cross-country route, demanding lengthy detours.) The return from Markarfljót to Reykjavík is then 126 km by the direct route.

Including travel from and back to Reykjavík, this is a journey of nearly 500 km. It is clearly too much for one day, bearing in mind that some of the roads are unsurfaced and weather could be unpropitious. Also, of course, you will want to stop and look around. The most comfortable solution is to spend at least one, ideally two, nights within the region in hotels such as those at Geysir, Flúðir, Rangá or Hvolsvöllur (though smaller hotels, B+B-equivalent 'farm holidays' and camping options also exist). Some links to websites for finding accommodation are provided on the Dorothy Dunnett Society website. You could, however, also cover the ground in two (or more) separate day trips from Reykjavík, breaking the itinerary and picking it up again somewhere like Flúðir.

South-West Iceland

Nicholas's conjectural route

Area covered by section map

Papey, Horn and Dyrhólaey

The Vatachino ship made its first landfalls on the Icelandic coast at Papey, Horn and Dyrhólaey.

Papey is over 400 km east of the Markarfljót river estuary and you should allow two days to get there from Markarfljót or three days from Reykjavík. Accommodation is available at or near all the locations. From Papey you may either return the same way, or complete the ring around Iceland via the Akureyri/Myvatn area in the north and continue on back to Reykjavík. That remaining section can be driven comfortably in two days, but allowing more time is better to enjoy the many attractions. This northern

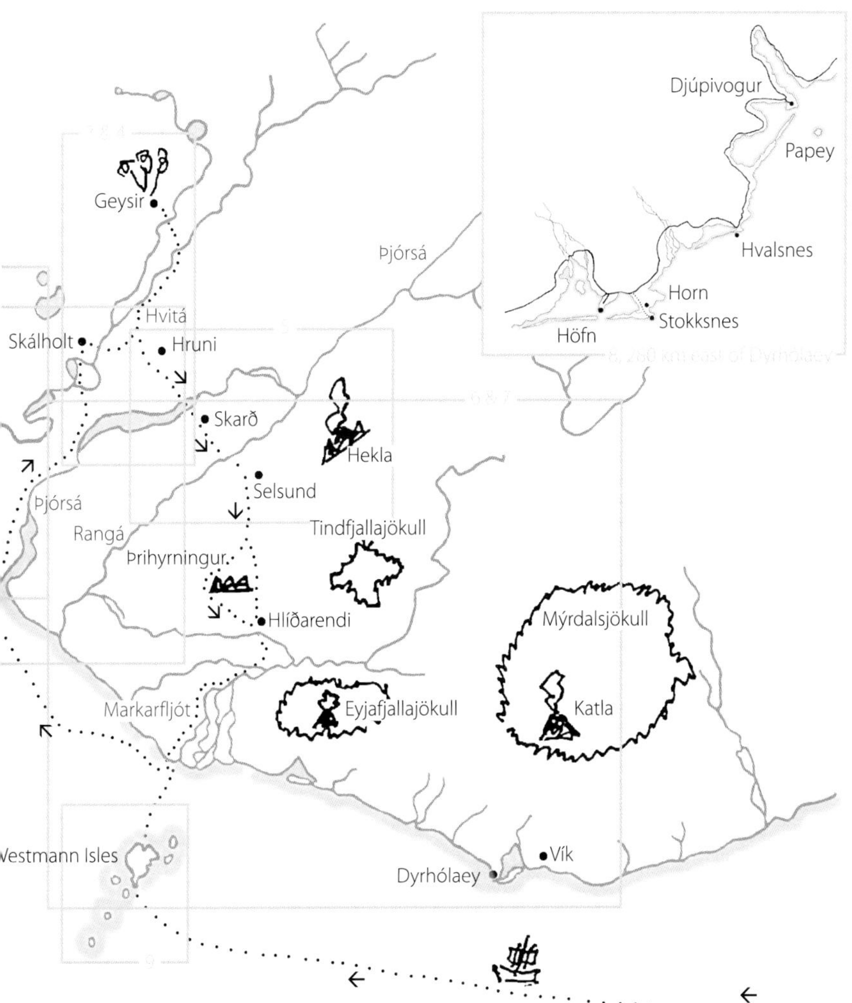

section of the Ring Road (Road N1) is not described in this guide as Dorothy Dunnett's characters do not venture there.

The diagram of distances and road numbers (not exactly to scale) on page 3 above illustrates all these options. To complete the whole itinerary starting from Reykjavík, a minimum of three to five days is advised; to cover the more remote sites and perhaps complete the ring around the country, up to eight to ten days; and add one or more days for the Westmann Isles if wished.

Vestmannaeyjar (The Westmann Isles)

If you wish to visit the Westmann Isles, first port of call for the *Svipa*, please check the travel options as they vary from year to year. You should allow at least an extra day for such a visit, and can find overnight accommodation in the town of Heimaey if needed.

A Little History

> *Everyone in Iceland knew who his ancestors were. Every farm, every hill, every rock had its name and its story. (*TLWL, *Ch 25)*

Lying nearly 1,000 km to the west of Norway, Iceland was the last outpost of Europe to be permanently colonised. Place names suggest that Celtic monks and hermits were the first to settle some of its lonely islands and promontories. The first large-scale influx, however, began with the Norwegian Ingólfur Arnarson claiming land near Reykjavík in 874, and it continued up to around 930. Most immigrants were west Norwegian in origin, but many others had lived meanwhile in Norse-occupied parts of Ireland or the Scottish isles. The richer settlers brought – and continued to bring – foreign slaves for manual work, leaving a substantial Celtic imprint both on the nation's genes and its culture.

The Norse settlement's leaders were escaping from Norway's increasingly authoritarian earls and kings. They organised Iceland as a free 'commonwealth', with local chieftains known as *goðar* providing the first level of defence, administration and justice. The country was divided into four quarters each with its own local assembly or 'thing', and an Alþingi or national assembly was held annually at Þingvellir in the south-west. There in the year 1000, a collective decision was made to adopt Christianity as the official religion – with the proviso that individuals might follow certain pagan practices in private. Even so, the compromise did not come easily, as shown by the fact that Hjalti Skeggjason's pro-Christian poem calling the goddess Freyja a bitch (quoted in chapter 26 of *To Lie With Lions*) had got him outlawed at the Alþingi just one year before.

This struggle between the old and new religions, both in Iceland and in the Faroes where it peaked in 999, surely helped inspire Dorothy Dunnett's brilliant realisation of Thorfinn/Macbeth in *King Hereafter* as an individual torn as much between the two creeds as he was between his two names and political roles.

Classic Icelandic society lived on a knife-edge between respect for the law and settling issues by force, and the Alþingi itself triggered many bloody skirmishes. After a relatively peaceful 12th century, the 'Age of the Sturlungs' saw a brutal civil war develop between magnates expanding their regional fiefdoms. By 1262, national leaders were driven to ask the Norwegian monarch to intervene and restore order. His rule was gradually asserted through a royal governor, but leaving the Alþingi in place; and this 'colonial' situation persisted until 1944 when Iceland declared its full independence. Meanwhile, however, the sovereign power shifted from Norway to Denmark following the union of their crowns at Kalmar in 1379. Copenhagen's strategic and commercial grip on Iceland was tighter at some times, looser at others, and from the late 19th century the Icelanders won successively higher degrees of self-government within the Danish realm.

Always a small country in power terms (with just 320,000 inhabitants today), Iceland

A typical Icelandic black beach at Reynisfjara near Vík

has punched above its weight culturally thanks to the sagas: manuscripts created from the 13th century onwards but referring to events two centuries earlier. Some can be confidently ascribed to authors like Snorri Sturlason, who also wrote other histories and treatises, but most reflected oral traditions built up over generations. One of the greatest sagas, the story of Burnt Njál, was played out over the same part of southern Iceland visited by Nicholas's party, who learned about it from their Icelandic hosts as they went. It figures later in this guide.

Nicholas's Era: the 'English Century'

The 15th century, when Nicholas came to Iceland, was a 'dark age' for cultural life including the writing of annals. The Black Death struck twice, killing up to half the population each time. Yet this period also saw the first blossoming of the fishing trade that has underpinned the Icelandic economy ever since, accounting today for some 40% of exports by value. Since the late 14th century the spring cod fishery had been drawing a regular migration of farmers and labourers to the western and southern coasts, where they camped on the beaches in simple huts of turf and driftwood, and fished with baited lines from boats carrying from two to twelve men. The catch was processed on land mainly as stockfish, and much of it was traded to foreign merchants in return for grain, clothing and other European luxuries. Further Icelandic exports were birds of prey for falconry, sulphur for making gunpowder and medicines, and woollen cloth (*wadmal*) – exactly as explained in *To Lie With Lions*.

Also as depicted by Dorothy Dunnett, this trade was lucrative enough to spur energetic and sometimes violent competition. Technically, only the Danish Crown could grant licences for ships to visit Iceland; and Danish policy was that all such trade must pass through Bergen in Norway, where it was dominated by Hanseatic merchants from Lübeck. Danish regulations also limited the size of boats the Icelanders themselves should use, hence the significance of Nicholas's gift of a larger 'dogger'. However, during the 15th century English traders intruded so forcefully that they regularly sent ten or more ships a year to the Icelandic fishing grounds, building fortified camps on the Westmann Isles to protect their catch. The rocky islands made a useful base because large vessels could not anchor directly on the flat and marshy 'double coasts' of the mainland, where outer sand-spits enclosed shallow lagoons before the shore proper. The visiting ships not only bought from the locals but lifted cod directly, salting it on board. For the most part the Icelandic fishermen were happy to cooperate, enjoying fair prices and the wide range of goods provided in return. For Icelandic historians, the expression 'English century' that became attached to the period as a result still carries largely positive overtones.

The problem lay in the competition. Denmark did not always turn a blind eye, and in 1467 – just five years before Nicholas's fictional visit – a party of English merchants were provoked to attack and kill the Danish governor Björn Thorleifsson in his house (now the Icelandic president's home) at Bessastaðir, carrying off all his treasures. For this and other reasons England was actually at war with Denmark from 1468–73, with the Hanseatic League joining the Danish side. From about 1470 German ships started sailing directly from Hamburg to take up fish for the British and continental market, while vessels from the Low Countries are also mentioned. In 1490 the Danish king made a treaty with England granting licences for English ships, and the Icelandic Alþingi passed a law requiring the German and English merchants to coexist peacefully – and never to over-winter in Iceland. Both provisions seem to have been cheerfully ignored, and in 1532 the worst fish-related battle yet took place between two English ships and a German one (backed by the locals) at Básendar on the south-west coast. This time the Germans won.

As the 16th century progressed, both the English interest and the sharpness of competition began to fade. The dynamics of the fish trade shifted as salt became available in bulk from southern Europe, allowing fish to be both fresh-salted and processed as 'clip-fish' or 'bacalao' (*saltfiskur* in Icelandic) – i.e. fish that is gutted and salted or soaked in brine, then laid out to dry on rocks. Icelandic production also shifted to the latter, although stockfish is still prepared today on large drying-racks and in slatted huts, providing 8% of Icelandic fish exports. So, Nicholas's visit in the *Svipa* was well-timed to catch the international competition over Icelandic cod at one of its peaks.[2]

Land of Ice and Fire

Iceland's extremes of 'ice and fire' have always fascinated foreigners, especially through their uncanny combinations – volcanoes erupting through an ice-cap, boiling water spurting through snow at Geysir in winter. Both features are ultimately linked to the country's geographical position. Low year-round temperatures have preserved permanent ice-fields since the last Ice Age on some 11% of Iceland's territory, The main such area, Vatnajökull, is also Europe's largest, covering 8,000 sq km with a maximum depth of 900 m. Several smaller ice-fields frame the zone of Nicholas's journey – Eyjafjallajökull and Mýrdalsjökull (the home of Katla) to the east, Langjökull to the north-west beyond Geysir, and Hofsjökull to the north-east. Smaller ice-caps form on the highest volcanoes.

The eruption at Eyjafjallajökull

Tindfjallajökull is an example in our area, while the 1,833-m-high Snæfellsjökull in the west is famed as the doorway for Jules Verne's *Journey to the Centre of the Earth* and as a supposed holy or mystical mountain. The same word *jökull* – roughly pronounced *yuk-ootl* – is used in Iceland both for these large ice-fields and for smaller ice tongues (outlet glaciers) flowing down from them, several of which can be seen (and sometimes reached by car) when driving along the south coast.

Museums about *jöklar* (the plural of *jökull*) exist at Höfn in the south-east and, on a smaller scale, at Skaftafell in the mid-south (both within the scope of this guide). There is a museum about sea-ice – which touches Iceland's north-west and north coasts in colder winters and provides the route for polar bears to enter the country – at Blönduós on road N1 in the north.

Iceland's natural fires are today interpreted as a result of plate tectonics, a process whereby huge interlocking segments of the earth's land and sea surface drift slowly over the molten inner layers. The theory itself was partly inspired by observations of a cleft running underwater down the middle of the North Atlantic Ocean with ridges on both sides, which is now understood as a 'productive margin' between the American and Eurasian plates. Hot magma (liquid rock) welling up there as a result of convection currents in the earth's interior has the effect of constantly pushing the plates out sideways and slowly widening the Atlantic. Simply put, Iceland is where this Mid-Atlantic Ridge comes up across dry land: the lavas extruded through the split have built up the country in stages and are still creating new land in its centre, pushing the western and eastern coasts further apart by around one inch per year.

To the south-west of Iceland the Mid-Atlantic Ridge splits in two, so it enters the

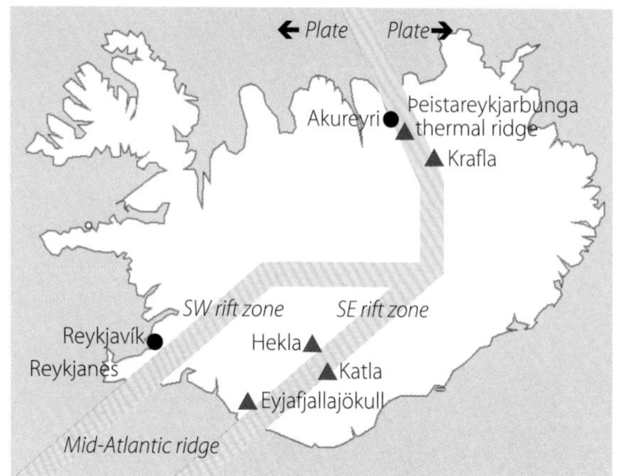

country both through the south-western peninsula of Reykjanes (where Keflavík Airport now stands) and through the south coast below Mount Hekla. Joining up around the middle of the country, it departs across the north coast near the northern capital of Akureyri. All Iceland's active volcanoes lie within this inverted and slanted Y-shape, as do the most active hot spring areas (geothermal fields). However, geothermal areas are scattered through the rest of the country and are increasingly exploited for energy generation, especially in the heavily populated south-west. The famous Blue Lagoon spa at Svartsengi near Keflavík is built upon spill-water from a power plant exploiting steam from an underground hotspot, and the complex includes a geothermal information centre, 'Gjáinn'. A similar display is at the new geothermal power plant 'Hellisheiðarvirkjun', just east of Reykjavík, on Road N1 (South) – see the route below from Reykjavík to Fljótshólar.

The price Icelanders pay for this exciting environment includes both eruptions and frequent earthquakes, which are most common along the lines of the Mid-Atlantic Ridge and below certain branching faults. Earthquake clusters often precede and accompany volcanic outbreaks, though the science of interpreting them for early warning is still developing. They can also – as depicted in *To Lie With Lions* – suck the force out of hot springs and make new ones burst out of the ground:

> *They were almost midstream … [when] with a rumbling crash a jet of steam rose in the air … Thick as the trunk of a tree, the cascade stood in the heart of the river. (*TLWL, *Ch 29)*

Of 30 volcanic sites still considered active in Iceland, 13 are known to have erupted since settlement times, producing one third of the whole world's output of lava over the last 500 years. The most regular performers are Hekla itself, which became the default example of vulcanism for medieval Europe and was suspected of being hell's mouth, and Grimsvötn under the western stretch of Vatnajökull. Hekla has erupted at least 20 times since the settlement, and once per decade in the late 20th century. Katla has had 21 recorded eruptions, the last major one in 1918. Eyjafjallajökull, notorious for its extended ash-rich eruption in 2010 and the consequent disruption of air traffic, is actually powered by a separate hot-spot alongside the main ridge. The 2010 events are now commemorated with an interesting film and exhibits at a small museum off the Road 1 (Ring Road) at Þorvaldseyri, east of the Markarfljót, while museums covering vulcanism in general are found at Stykkishólmur on Snæfellsenes in the west and at Geysir.

As Iceland's towns have been built at a prudent distance from volcanoes (except on the Westmann Isles), few lives have ever been lost by the direct effects of explosions and lava. The worst killers have been volcanic gases, dust and ash, which in the case of Laki's 1783–4 eruption are thought to have killed some 50% of the livestock and (through famine) 25% of human inhabitants. The second most destructive side-effects are the floods of sulphur-laced water and mud set off by eruptions underneath ice-caps, which in the south pour down to the coast with dramatic force, rolling huge ice-blocks with them and shattering even the most modern infrastructures. These events have the generic name of 'jökulhlaup' – usually translated 'glacier burst' – and in recent years they have repeatedly swept away bridges and parts of the National Ring Road between the Markarfljót estuary and Skaftafell.

A simultaneous eruption of Hekla and Katla, as witnessed by Nicholas and his friends in *To Lie With Lions*, would thus have been horrendous indeed. The one small snag is that these two volcanoes are never known to have erupted at the same time, and the closest reported Hekla eruptions to the time of *Svipa's* visit were in 1440 and 1510. No activity at all in Katla is known from the late 15th century. True, given poor annals-keeping, only five eruptions across Iceland were recorded for the whole century compared with eleven in the 14th century and fifteen in the 16th; so it is plausible that some events went unreported or the records were lost. Further, a buried layer of ash in the Markarfljót and Rangá areas suggests an unreported eruption of Hekla that some experts have placed around 1490.

But there is a further problem about the double eruption. The view towards Katla from the Hvítá, Þjórsá, and Rangá river valleys, and from the Markarfljót estuary and neighbouring seas, is blocked by the intervening mass of the volcano Eyjafjallajökull and the ridge of Tindfjallajökull, both higher than Katla as well as substantially closer. Only on the last leg of their trek from Selsund to Hlíðarendi might Nicholas and Kathi have been able to climb high enough to glimpse Katla at times. We might concede that the warning columns of smoke rising from both volcanoes could be seen at once, even with the actual peak of Katla blocked; but Icelandic eruptions typically start explosively, with the 'smoke' (actually ash and steam) coming afterwards from pulverised rock and vaporised ice. Once the eruptions began, both ash-clouds could have been visible from a single vantage point on land or at sea, but the geography would still not allow both craters to be seen simultaneously, with such dramatic touches as ice being thrown in the air (itself unlikely). In fact, Dorothy Dunnett's apocalyptic vision of these disasters would make more sense geologically if the second eruption had been in Eyjafjallajökull, which rises directly above the Markarfljót river estuary and is visible from far to the west. Eyjafjallajökull and Katla have three times erupted in close succession and are easily confused by visitors to Iceland even today; so we might credit Dorothy Dunnett with knowingly conflating them – and/or Tindfjallajökull? – for maximum impact.

The Land Itinerary

Nicholas's itinerary is presented section by section below, in the order most naturally followed when starting from Reykjavík. Thus the Markarfljót river estuary is described last as it lies furthest east, even though *Svipa* first anchored there. The locations cannot always be presented in the order visited in *To Lie With Lions* because of the long detours mentioned in the introduction to this guide; but it is hoped that the quotations will help place them in context. Many parts of Nicholas's route – especially after Geysir – are also conjectural; but the reasoning behind all guesses made is explained, and everyone is welcome to seek better solutions.

The overland journey began at the Þjórsá estuary. Nicholas reported to his companions that Anselm and Kathi left Markarfljót where he had deposited them 'and set off by sea to the mouth of the Thjórsá.' (*TLWL*, chapter 25). Nicholas and Benecke follow the same route.

The first section therefore guides you the 90 km or so from Reykjavík to the farm at Fljótshólar, the nearest settlement to the landing site at the Þjórsá estuary.

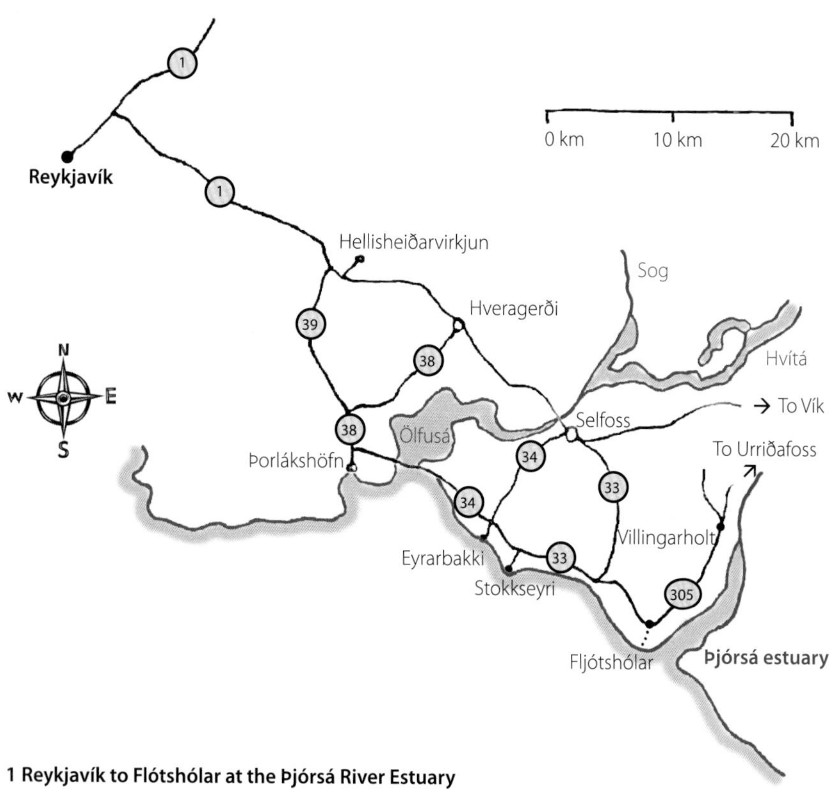

1 Reykjavík to Flótshólar at the Þjórsá River Estuary

Getting to the Start:

1 Reykjavík to Fljótshólar at the Þjórsá River Estuary

Starting from Reykjavík, you will need to take the N1 (South) and drive in the direction of Vík, mounting up into the plateau of Hellisheiði amid dramatic mountains and lava-fields. From here you can choose between two routes.

For the first, shorter, route look out for a right turn (before the main plateau) on to Road 39 signposted to Eyrarbakki, Stokkseyri and Þorlákshöfn. This offers a short cut to the south coast over the Þrengsli pass, a truly dramatic drive though tricky in snow or slippery conditions. On descending to level ground the road number changes to 38 after a junction with the road coming south from Hveragerði (described below). Four kilometres later, turn left onto Road 34 towards Eyrarbakki and Stokkseyri, while Road 38 continues ahead to the ferry port of Þorlákshöfn. You will now continue pretty much in a straight line towards Fljótshólar (see further route details below).

Alternatively, continue on Road N1 towards Hveragerði. You may like to visit the geothermal power display centre at Hellisheiðarvirkjun just off to the left before the final climb to the plateau. From the heights, the road descends in wide curves to the town of Hveragerði, famous for its thermally-heated greenhouses. As you reach the western edge of the town there is a roundabout where Road 1 continues ahead to the larger town of Selfoss. Here you turn right on Road 38 (marked to Þorlákshöfn), from where in good weather you have a constant view of snow-topped Eyjafjallajökull far to the east. After 11.5 km on Road 38 you will pass, on your right, the junction with Road 39 coming from Reykjavík over Þrengsli pass (just described). The two alternative routes converge here and, as above, you should turn left after 4 km on to Road 34 heading initially for Eyrarbakki and Stokkseyri. The expanse of water now on your left is the estuary of the Ölfusá river, formed by the confluence, north of Selfoss, of the Hvítá with the Sog river. The estuary is a haven for migrating birds, and the dunes along the sea-coast to your right (known as the 'Flói' area) are a nature reserve.

Driving 33 km due east, the road number changes from 34 to 33 and then 305, which brings you to the Þjórsá's mouth. Along the way, you will drive past Eyrarbakki and then through Stokkseyri. These towns developed as trading places and fishing ports mainly during the 19th century, when their harbours were improved. Eyrarbakki has a local museum in a wooden merchant's house, Húsið, and a maritime museum next to it; while Stokkseyri boasts a museum of wildlife and hunting, and a tongue-in-cheek museum of Icelandic ghosts and myths, 'Draugasetrið'. Their fish restaurants are popular with visitors and Icelanders alike.

Off Stokkseyri and further east the shore is made picturesque by lava formations. Most evocative in relation to *To Lie With Lions* is a site called Þuríðarbúð on the eastern outskirts of Stokkseyri – to the right as you exit along Road 33 – where a replica has been created of a 19th-century fisherman's hut. It is named after Þuríður Einarsdóttir, a local woman (1777–1863) who dressed and worked as a man, flourishing as a fisherman for 25 years. If one imagines something even smaller, rougher and smokier, this grass-roofed building and the information about fishermen's customs attached to it may give a glimpse of the 15th-century fishing camps at Markarfljót.

> *... humped grassy mounds, which were also cabins, built of rock stuffed with grass and roofed with turf. Round about them were the fish-cleaning trestles, the vats*

of unspeakable offal, and the wind-huts where the grey fish were drying. (TLWL, *Ch 25)*

Urriðafoss on Þjórsá

To complete this section of the route to the mouth of the Þjórsá, continue eastward from Stokkseyri on Road 33 (marked to Selfoss), then bear right on to Road 305 marked Villingarholt. From this junction until you rejoin Road N1 the road has a dirt surface but is mostly flat, sufficiently wide and an easy drive. Some 15 km east of Stokkseyri you will reach the farm of Fljótshólar, where Road 305 curves to the left to follow the course of the river north.

Fljótshólar at the Þjórsá River Estuary

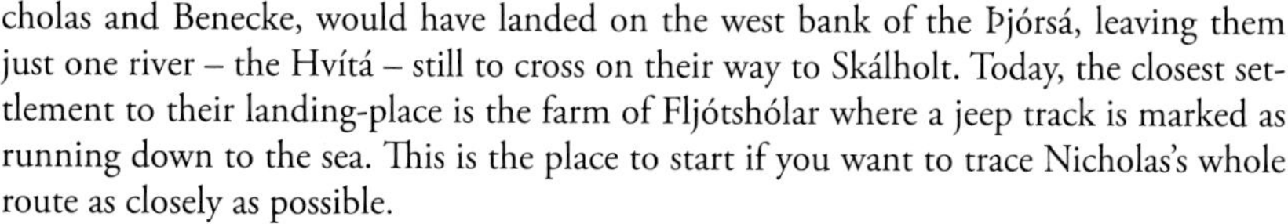

Both parties, Anselm and Kathi and Nicholas and Benecke, would have landed on the west bank of the Þjórsá, leaving them just one river – the Hvítá – still to cross on their way to Skálholt. Today, the closest settlement to their landing-place is the farm of Fljótshólar where a jeep track is marked as running down to the sea. This is the place to start if you want to trace Nicholas's whole route as closely as possible.

THE ÞJÓRSÁ

The Þjórsá is Iceland's longest river and flows for 237 km from a source under Hofsjökull to the north-east of the *To Lie With Lions* zone to reach the sea near Þykkvabær in *Njal's Saga* country. Its name has been traced to a Gaelic loan-word 'tarbh' meaning 'bull' (cf Latin *taurus*). For much of its upper course Þjórsá is narrow and fast-running and it has only been bridged twice: where the Ring Road (1) crosses it at Þjórsártún in the south, and far to the north where it meets Road 32 beyond Búrfell. Several fords are, however, recorded on its middle course around Árnes where it is punctuated by islands. Þjórsá has many waterfalls including, on its upper course, ones with such colourful names as Thief's Falls and the Troll-woman's Leap. Urriðafoss just south of the Ring Road has a greater throughput of water even than Gullfoss or the mighty Dettifoss in the north. The obstacle created by the Þjórsá together with the baleful influence of Hekla on the surrounding areas have kept its banks more barren and thinly populated than those of the Hvítá throughout history. Today, however, it enjoys economic significance through the damming of its waters at numerous places for hydroelectric power. Of the five such stations already working, two, Búrfellsstöð and Sultartangastöð, are passed on the section of our route from Flúðir to Skarð (below). Another is due to be completed at the end of 2013 and at least three others are mooted, but have triggered debate over whether the river's whole natural character risks being lost.

2 Fljótshólar to Skálholt

In their pursuit of Anselm and Kathi, Nicholas and Benecke picked up horses here to ride to Skálholt.

As Nicholas's own party rode

> *... on each side was a lava-field, and on top, sepia and white, lay the boulders and blocks which had not been created or tossed there by man. And beyond that were the heights ... [and] so transparently clear was the air that the eastern glaciers lay, rank upon rank, as if iced on the blue of the sky ... In the lands that he knew there was no terrain like this ... Nor such golden, golden light.* (TLWL, *Ch 25)*

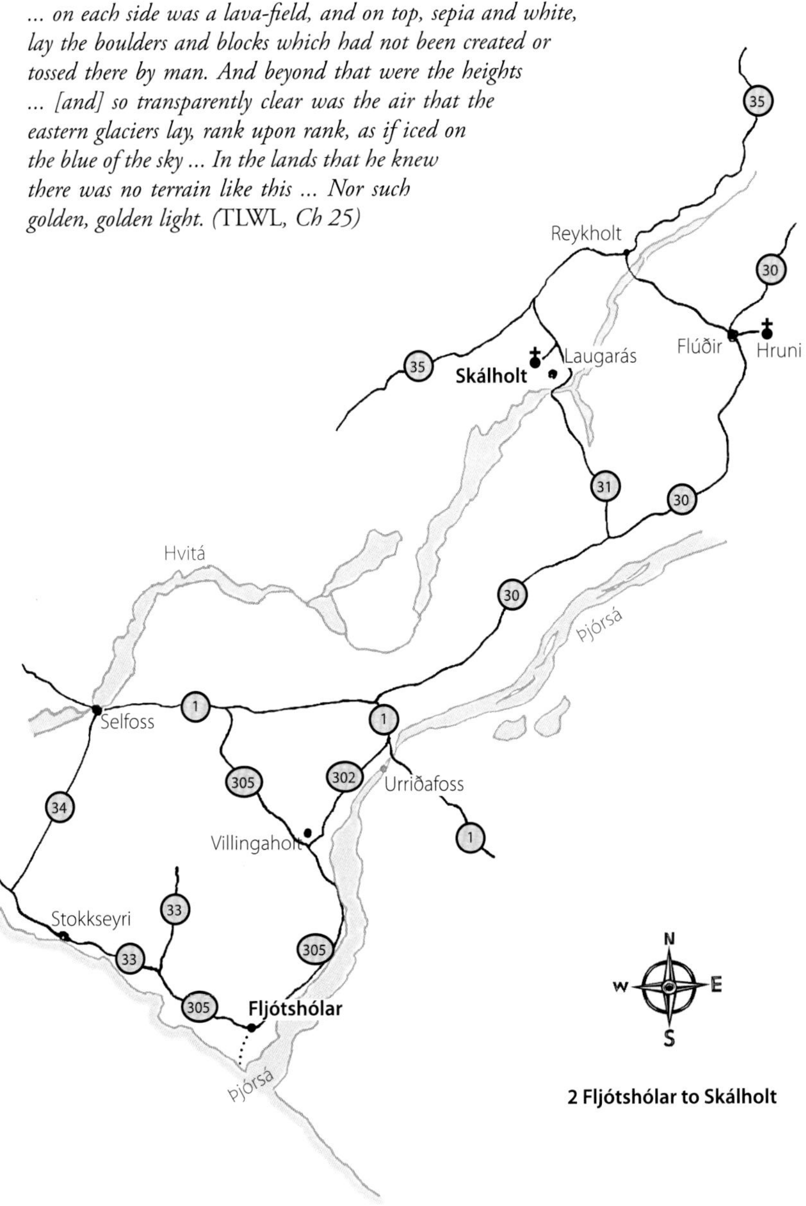

2 Fljótshólar to Skálholt

Your route is Road 305 northwards alongside the river from Fljótshólar. After 13 km turn right on to Road 302 marked Urriðafoss (there is a large building on the left at this junction called Flórskóli).

A few kilometres further along the road surface gets worse but there are good views of the Þjórsá to the right. On this stretch, just before re-joining Road N1, you can turn right to a parking place at the waterfall Urriðafoss (Trout Falls), Iceland's largest in terms of the volume of water flow.

We cannot tell where Nicholas's group struck out westwards from the Þjórsá valley to cut across to the Hvítá and Skálholt, but modern roads allow you to make the journey quite directly. When Road 302 makes a T-junction with Road N1 (the ring road), turn left and follow the N1 for 2 km to reach the junction with Road 30. Here you turn right, following signs northward to Geysir, Flúðir and Skálholt.

After 17 km turn left on to Road 31 marked to Skálholt and Geysir. The long mountain now on your left is called Vörðufell, and facing you on the horizon is the often snow-capped Miðdalsfjall mountain range that runs from the north-east of Lake Þingvallavatn towards Geysir. After 10 km you reach a bridge over the Hvítá erected in 1957, called Iðubrú, which replaces the Iða ferry that Nicholas's party used when going both to and from Skálholt.

Dorothy Dunnett describes the river here when Nicholas leaves Skálholt in pursuit of Kathi (see next section):

> *It was an unpleasant river: broad, and plated with grey and white at the edges. The running currents were not at once apparent; in places the surface was turgid, or mixed with the chopped and scurrying pools of the frustrated flow.* (TLWL, *Ch 26)*

Beyond the bridge lies the modern village of Laugarás with its geothermally-heated greenhouses. Drive through it and up the hill beyond. Skálholt lies immediately on the left. Make sure that you take the turning marked 'Skálholt' with various graphics rather than an earlier one saying 'Skálholtsbýli', etc., which leads to a more private area including the bishop's home.

THE HVÍTÁ

Iceland's third longest river runs for 185 km if its final stretch Ölfusá (from the confluence with the Sog down to the coast) is included. Literally the 'White River', the Hvítá originates more than 900 m above sea level under the ice-cap of Langjökull, emerging as a substantial stream from Lake Hvítárvatn on Langjökull's north-east flank. It is therefore called a glacial river – as distinct from a spring-fed 'mountain' river – but has many non-glacial tributaries, so its water is not too turbid or greenish. Its seasonal flow varies greatly depending on the weather and speed of glacier melting, and it has caused emergencies in the past by breaking its banks. In early spring a 'step-flood' can be caused when melt-water builds up behind a natural dam of ice and debris, then floods the next part of the canyon when it breaks through. The Hvítá has not been, historically, a major obstacle for Icelandic life, as it is easily forded in most stretches to as far north as the bridge at Brúarhlöð (see below). Before modern bridges, the best-known fords were at Steypuvað, Kópsvatnsvað and Ísabakkavað among others.

Modern Skálholt under snow

Skálholt

Spread over a flat hill-top with commanding views, Skálholt became the seat of the first Icelander to be papally consecrated – in 1056 – as a bishop for Iceland. This was Ísleifr, son of Gissur the White, the same who features in *King Hereafter*, and he made Skálholt his see because his grandfather, Teitur, first settled there. Iceland's southern bishopric remained here until 1800 (with the northern see at Hólar, south of Akureyri), punctuated by dramas such as the murder of a foreign bishop by locals in 1433 and the killing of the last Catholic bishop, Jón Árason, and his sons in 1550.

Today's Skálholt is dominated by its modern cathedral built in 1956 on the summit of the hill, with the seminary and residential buildings grouped below to the west. The visitor centre, restaurant and guesthouse are also on this side by the main car park. The cathedral interior houses a 13th-century bishop's tomb and an ecclesiastical museum, with *inter alia* a copy of the first printed Bible in Icelandic (from the 1560s). Alongside the cathedral a replica has been built of 'Þorláksbuð', the very modest church of one of the early bishops – a gabled wooden structure reinforced with rough stone walls and roofed with turf.

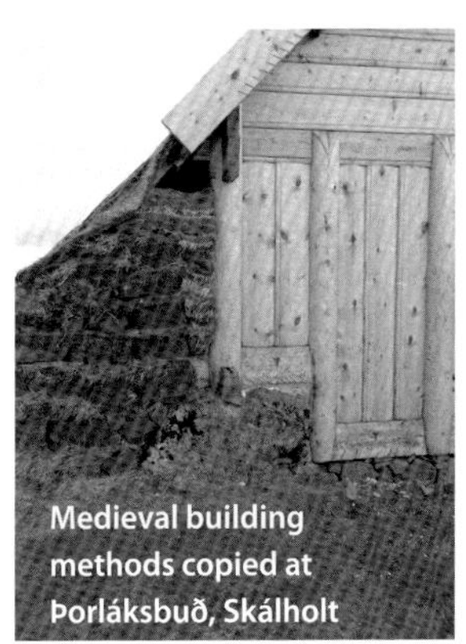
Medieval building methods copied at Þorláksbuð, Skálholt

... the guest-quarters of the Bishop's Cathedral at Skálholt, which was a collection of snow-plastered buildings surrounding a handsome small church made of wood. The roofs were of much-nibbled grass covered with footmarks, and blackened and singed from the smoke from the kitchen. There was no fire in Kathi's room, which contained a standing bed and a chest and a basin ... (TLWL, *Ch 26)*

Below the modern cathedral to the south, excavations in 2002–7 have exposed the foundations of the historic settlement in its 18th-century layout, including an underground passage that leads from the out-buildings into the church crypt – doubtless a boon during blizzards! The *To Lie With Lions* visitor can try to guess where travellers like Nicholas and the Sersanders siblings would have been housed.

3 Skálholt to Geysir (and Gullfoss)

When Nicholas, Benecke and Glímu-Sveinn left Skálholt to track Anselm, Kathi and Sigfús on their falcon-hunt turned bear-hunt, they re-crossed the Hvítá and then would presumably have ridden north straight up the east bank. There is no road that follows the east bank closely so, to avoid too much doubling-back, we shall instead take a road to the west of the river as far as Geysir. For this, we continue west from Skálholt on Road 31, then turn right on Road 35, just by the bridge over the Brúará river (a tributary of the Hvítá). This leads up through horse-breeding country and the small town of Reykholt, which also has greenhouses exploiting thermal energy. To the north in good weather you should by now see clearly the inland ice-cap Langjökull, fringed on the left by the spiky Jarlshettur mountains and with the single large mountain Bláfell on the right. Closer on the left looms the dark gravel mountain of Bjarnarfell under which Geysir lies. Geysir is reached after a total of 28 km from Skálholt.

Geysir

> *'Hot springs,' Nicholas [said]. 'Great big enormous hot gushers, leaping a hundred feet high. Bubbling mud. Steaming pools. Seething rivers. They're all over Iceland. People cook their food in them, and dry and wash their clothes, and bathe themselves every … Saturday.' (*TLWL*, Ch 26)*

The hot spring 'Strokkur' at Geysir

When arriving by car one may park either at the main visitor complex which includes a hotel, café, a huge shop and an exhibition, or at a side gate on the Haukadalur road to the north-east. The exhibition has a film loop of a Great Geysir eruption and much information on volcanoes and earthquakes, plus a small farming display on the upper floor.

The high-spurting springs of Geysir have given their name to similar phenomena all over the world, but the word in Icelandic simply means 'gusher' and is not even the site's correct original name. That would be Haukadalur (Hawk Valley), from the name of the farm founded here in the 10th century, which was linked with the family of Bishop Ísleifr (his son Teitur established a school here), and was

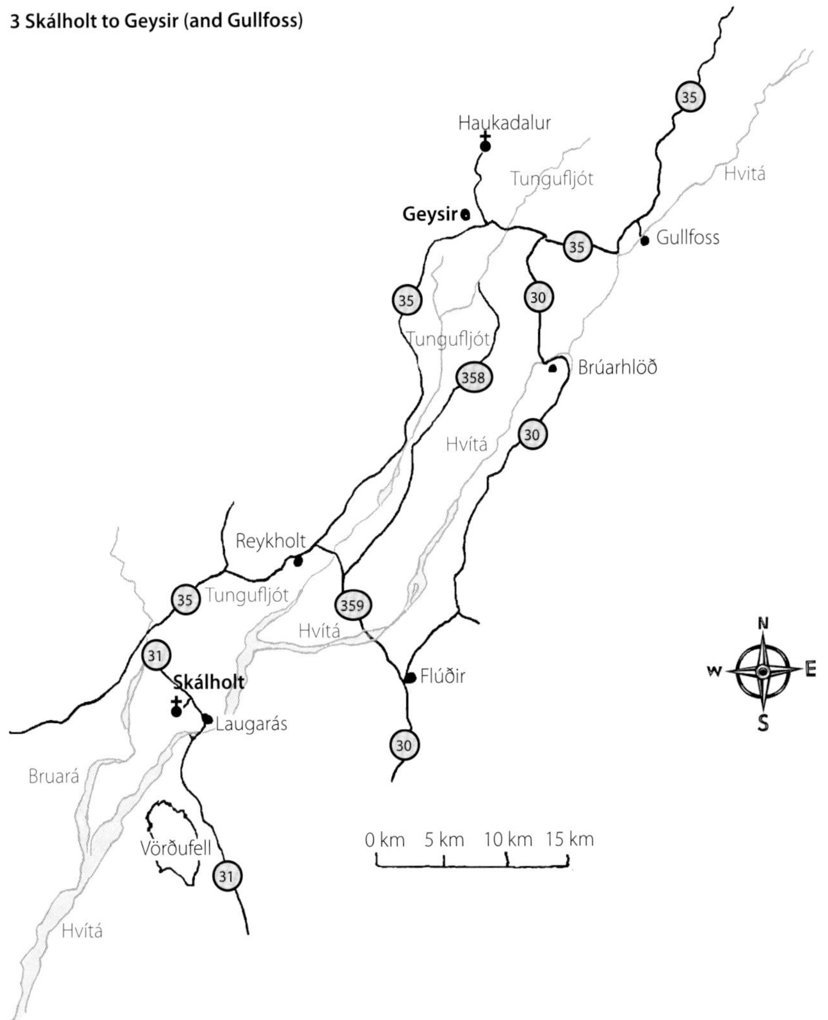

finally abandoned in 1938. A church still stands, founded in 1030 but most recently rebuilt in the 19th century: the woods around it suggest how different the countryside must have looked before sheep and climate fluctuations ravaged the vegetation.

The thermal field itself is a high-temperature area and at 3 sq km, one of the smaller ones in Iceland, owing its fame rather to accessibility and the drama of its largest springs. It lies approximately 120 m above sea level on the western arm of the inverted Y-shape of Iceland's volcanic ridge. Active for at least 7,000 years, the Geysir hot-spot has shifted its positions southwards over time and fluctuated in strength as a result of earthquakes. Curiously, in the 1890s the surrounding land was bought by an English speculator who charged an entry fee, but in 1935 ownership reverted to an Icelander, who gifted it to the nation. Well before that, the site had become a must for foreign visitors, who regularly camped there and experimented (like Anselm and Kathi Sersanders) with cooking their food in the boiling waters.

Gullfoss, part-frozen in March

The mechanism of Geysir's spouting springs is still not fully understood, but starts with rainwater seeping down to overheated layers of rock from an old volcanic centre, some 2 to 5 km below ground. The heated water pushes back up through fissures, and in passages of a certain shape experiences pressures that raise it to some 125 degrees centigrade. This causes a flash conversion into steam that forces its way out explosively. The most spectacular results were once seen at the Great Geysir, which spouted as high as 70 m; but it fell silent between 1900–1935 and today has to be coaxed artificially into erupting with 40 kg of soap. As this is only done on VIP occasions, most visitors make do with the smaller Strokkur spring which erupts every 8 to 10 minutes to a height of 30 to 35 m. Strokkur has also been choked up in the past by visitors trying to trigger it with stones and turf – so in playing with the springs as Dorothy Dunnett describes, Nicholas and his friends were setting a bad precedent. A re-drilling of the pipe in 1963 restored the spring to its present vigour.

The Geysir natural park contains many other interesting springs and pools, such as the deep blue Blesi pool and the so-called Little Geysir. Good views can be had from the hills behind, including the snowy summit of Hekla in good weather.

Gullfoss

Nine km north of Geysir on Road 35 is the waterfall Gullfoss. Even if not mentioned in *To Lie With Lions*, it is too good a sight to miss and involves only a trivial detour. Traffic is directed up to the left of the falls, following Road 35, to a platform with a visitor centre from which you walk down to the riverbank; but with your own car you may also continue straight ahead to a parking area giving a frontal view of the lower falls. Gullfoss is one of the two largest and most famous waterfalls in Iceland and the only noteworthy fall in the Hvítá. It descends by two slanted steps into the deep gorge of Hvítárgljúfur, running 40 to 70 m below the surrounding land. Over time, the river has not only eaten its way backwards into the rock ledges at the fall, but carved out different channels for itself both above and below. Gullfoss has only been accessible to visitors since the late 19th century when the surrounding roads were improved, but today is much sought-after both in summer and also in winter when the whole falls can freeze into an extraordinary ice cascade. Either way you can scramble over the rocks of the western bank for closer views but note that the surface can be treacherous in wet or frosty weather.

4 Geysir to Flúðir

This section travels south on Road 30 for about 22 km to Flúðir, a modern town that by definition does not feature in *To Lie With Lions* but provides a convenient staging-point (including overnight accommodation if wished).

On this segment we can look for sites mentioned in *To Lie With Lions*, both on Nicholas's initial route to Geysir and on the first stage of his return. First we will speculate on where the party crossed the Hvítá when heading for and coming from Geysir, described as a ferry-place but also fordable at a pinch. (Note that to get in and out of Geysir they would also have had to cross the Tungnaá/Tungufljót, but it appears that this moderate-sized river was not an obstacle worth mentioning.) Further south, we can look for the place on the river where the Sersanders group – on their own earlier route towards Geysir – tracked down and killed a female polar bear; and for their guide Sigfús's farm some 5 miles below the kill, to which he took the bear cub but which was later destroyed by an avalanche. On Nicholas's return journey, this was where he used divining to rescue both humans and the cub. Glímu-Sveinn's own farm is implied to lie not far from Sigfús's, as Anselm Sersanders was carried there (thus separating him from Nicholas's party) after breaking an ankle in the snow. Tentative identifications for all these sites are given in the sequence as they arise along the route below.

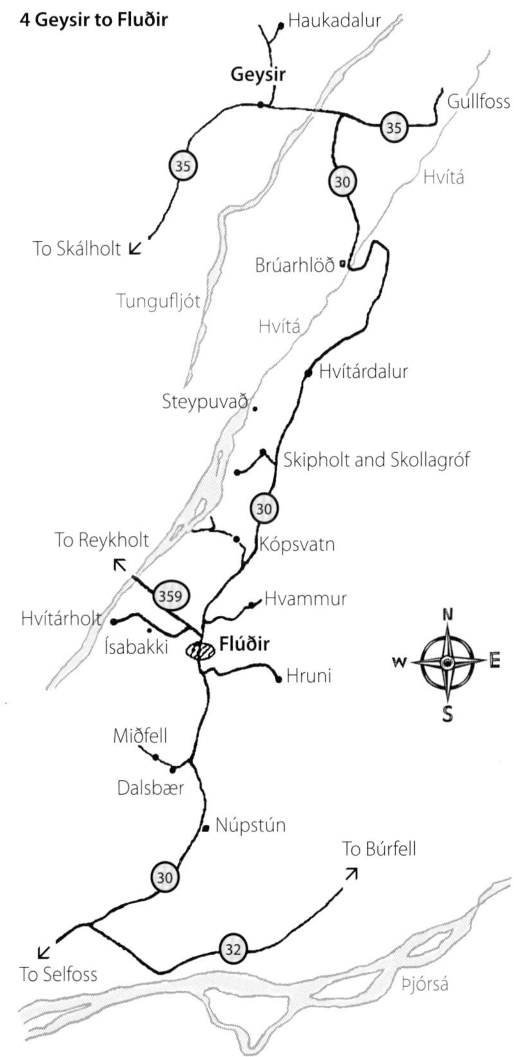

Continue on Road 35 from Geysir to the right turn onto Road 30 (or if returning from Gullfoss, turn left). There is a good dirt surface for the first 4 km of Road 30 and the rest is fully metalled. After 6 km we reach the modern bridge over the Hvítá at Brúarhlöð, literally

'The Pillar of the Bridge'. The name reflects a story that the rocks once formed a natural bridge, which was destroyed through a quarrel between local farmers. This picturesque spot is the most northerly point where it is possible to imagine Nicholas's team crossing, although it would mean they initially headed southeast from Geysir rather than due south. It would be a short distance for a ferry and there are wadeable channels both up and downstream.

Possible avalanche site at Miðfell farm near Flúðir

If the party instead headed due south, a more credible crossing-place on the Hvítá would be the historic ford and ferry-point of Steypuvað, some 10 km further south and to the west of Road 30. No track leads there today but you can work out where it lies – and try to hike there if wished, although this author has not tried it – by noting the farm Hvítárdalur on the right of the road 8.5 km south of Brúarhlöð, and continuing for about 1.5 km further. You can park the car on the roadside and will approach the river over rolling grass-covered ridges on the right.

This is also the most northerly place where the Hvítá starts to break up around islands, so could it also have been the place of the bear's fatal encounter?

> *Then they got to the river … this stretch of the Hvítá was wide, with … wide banks of sand which divided the fast, thrusting currents … [and at] the idling edge of the river … the thick milky water was marbled with blood. (*TLWL, *Ch 26)*

The bear's body is abandoned on an island, 'a bank of gritty black sand'.

If the bear-killing was indeed at or near Steypuvað, there are candidates nearby for Sigfús's and perhaps Glímu-Sveinn's farms. After a further 1.5 km along Road 30, look on the right of the road for a sign to Skipholt III and Skollagróf that leads by a short gravel track to two farms sheltering under escarpments to the west. (If you see 'Skipholt I' you have gone too far!) These slopes are not 'massive' but after heavy snow might have generated avalanches, especially if the old buildings lay closer under the rocks. It is, at any rate, an atmospheric site.

As the river flows south towards Flúðir, there are islands and relatively easy fording all the way down. Four to five km further south from the Skipholt turning, another known ford and possible bear-killing location can be reached by car at Kópsvatn. (Note: ignore the road on the left marked 'Hruni 5 km' – there is a better road south of Flúðir.) Turn right at Kópsvatn and drive past the farm and, later, an isolated barn to reach the river. The track is overgrown but manageable. If the bear was cornered here, Sigfús's farm could lie near Flúðir 5 km further on.

under snow in March

Flúðir

This pleasant small town offers an Icelandair hotel, a guesthouse/café and a supermarket with free toilets. The neighbourhood is full of rocky hills with many actual or potential sites for Sigfús's farm. The closest to town of these is Hvammur, which lies just north of Flúðir as you come in by Road 30 and is marked with a small sign to the left just before the road crosses a minor river. A dirt track, becoming quite rough, leads through thermal greenhouses with a basalt escarpment on the left, passing a mixture of new summer homes and older farms at Högnastaður and Hvammur I and II. These farms are close enough under the cliffs to have been exposed to avalanches. But if you would like to follow the track to its scenic end and imagine other possible sites, turn up left after the plant nursery (*plöntusala*) sign and before the dead-end road sign.

If Sigfús lived somewhere like this, Glímu-Sveinn could have chosen many other less exposed sites for his own farm. An intriguing one is the farm Hvítárholt on the bank of the Hvítá, north-west of Flúðir. Recent excavations of a Viking-age farm there unearthed a Roman coin, testimony to Iceland's early trading links. To reach Hvítárholt if *coming from* Flúðir, turn left from Road 30 just over 1 km north of Flúðir onto Road 359 (marked to Reykholt) then left at the first roundabout onto a road signposted to Hvítárholt and a golf course. After about 1.5 km look out for a set of small blue signs pointing right towards Hvítárholt and other farms. This is a somewhat bumpy dirt road that reaches the bank of Hvítá after about 1.5 km with the farm of Ísabakki on the left, and after another kilometre reaches and transits the farmyard at Hvítárholt before continuing along the river. As you drive from the Ísabakki farm towards Hvítárholt, the old Ísabakki fording place can be spotted at a gravelly area just after the road bends to run by the river, and provides a picturesque site for a possible picnic.

There are two more possible farm sites south of Flúðir, which could be visited when heading for Skarð (next section). A very picturesque possible avalanche site lies 3.5 km south of Flúðir on Road 30, where a sign points right 1 km to Miðfell. This is the largest of several farms nestling under high crags, where the slopes – now lushly wooded – show signs of earlier land- and rock-slides. Depending how far south you want to search, the old farm on the left some 2 or 3 km further south at Núpstún is also worth considering as a potential home for Sigfús or Glímu-Sveinn.

Hruni

Hruni, the ancient farm and church that Anselm and Kathi were heading for to hunt falcons until they ran into the polar bear with her cub, lies 5 km east of Flúðir. As Flúðir itself is some 9 to 10 km due east of Skálholt, it is likely that the Sersanders group were heading towards the modern town when they got diverted at the Hvítá. Nowadays, the best route for visiting Hruni from Flúðir is to take Road 30 south and just after leaving the town, look for Road 345 on the left, signposted to Hruni (3 km). This is a wide dirt road with some bad potholes, leading to a wooden church and parsonage best known for a legend about the flat-topped cliff alongside. Supposedly, Hruni church once stood proudly on the cliff, but the devil dragged it down into the ground with everyone inside as punishment for an orgy of dancing held there one Christmas night.

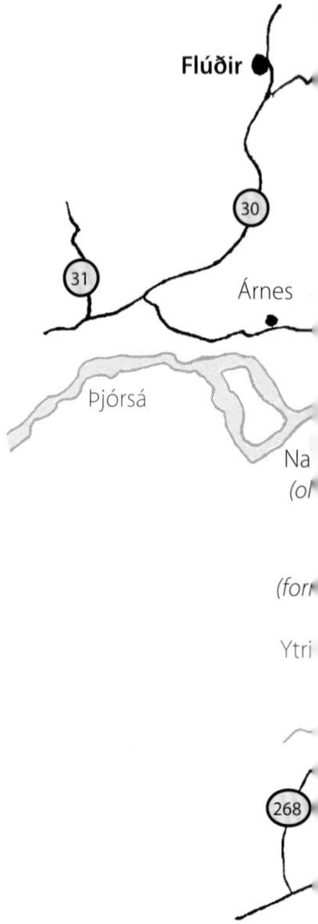

5 Flúðir to Skarð via the Þjórsá River Valley

This section of our itinerary takes us to the farm named Skarð, which is just east of the Þjórsá. After reaching the river our route takes a long detour northeastwards on its hither bank, forced by a lack of bridges, then south again on the other side of the Þjórsá to pick up Nicholas's trail. The cross-country journey would have been approximately 17 km, while ours will be some 70 km.

We start by continuing southwards on Road 30 from Flúðir for 13 km to the junction with Road 32, where we turn left. After less than 3 km we are reunited with the Þjórsá, here flowing broadly and calmly southwest, with Hekla coming back into view over to the east. This is a good place to start thinking about the location of the tiny basalt chapel where the group rested overnight. Seen from Robin's point of view as he waited at Markarfljót, Nicholas's party are said to be:

> *... forty miles to the north, in a basalt chapel the size of a hen-coop [and] it was ... just possible that they would reach Hlídarendi by the following evening. There was the Rangar river to cross, and its tributaries ... there was Hekla to pass, and then the jökull, the glacier which overlaid Katla ... That first killing stretch ... was to take them south to the farmhouse of Selsund, a halfway station where they could take time to rest ... after Selsund was passed, the basalt ridges and the bogs and the Markarfljót would hinder all progress. (*TLWL, *Ch 28)*

It is not easy to work out where Dorothy Dunnett envisaged the chapel. She implies that it is as far from Selsund as Selsund is from Hlíðarendi, and that it has an open view to the east and south. The distance cited would make Hruni itself a possible candidate, but it has no such open vistas anywhere nearby. Since the Rangá is mentioned as the main river needing to be crossed the next day, it might seem natural to assume that the travellers have already crossed the Þjórsá: but the chapel is also described as still well short of Skarð which is itself only 3 to 4 km beyond the Þjórsá. We may, therefore, also look at sites that meet the general criteria on the near (north-westerly) side of this river, and we will note them as we drive upstream.

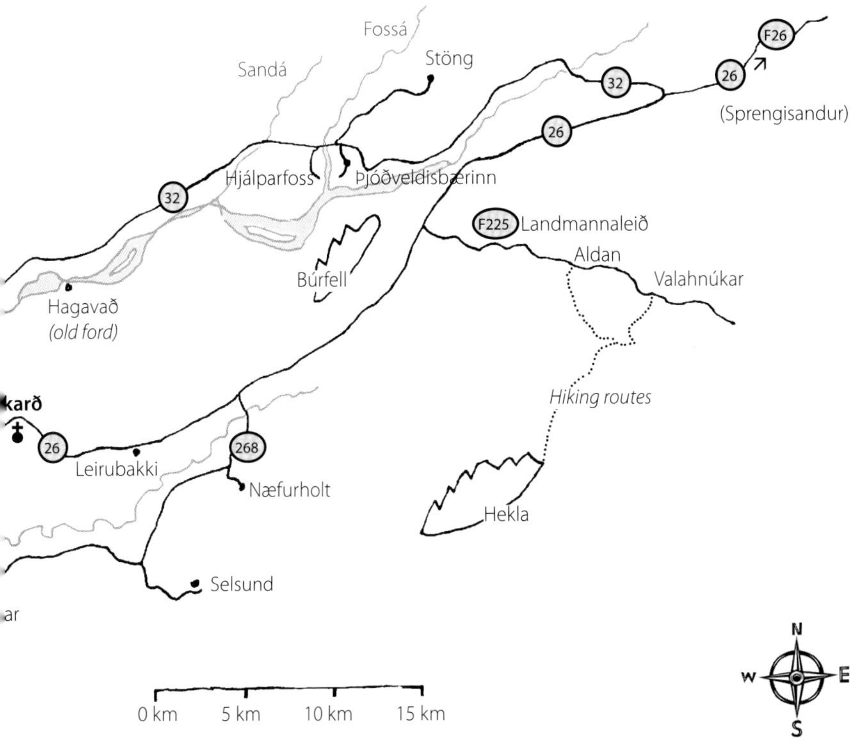

5 Flúðir to Skarð via the Þjórsá River Valley

Continuing northeastwards along Road 32, the first village along the way, Árnes, has a Þjórsá Visitors' Centre, 'Þjórsárstofa'. Just beyond it on the left is a fine example of a 'rétt', a large communal sheep-fold used to corral and identify different owners' animals when the sheep are driven down from the mountains in late September/October for their winter shelter. These autumn round-ups are popular events, with a chance to re-live old ways by tracking the sheep on horseback, and a great deal of alcohol-fuelled celebration.

Possible chapel sites on this bank of the Þjórsá can be imagined along the next section. One worth visiting is Stóri-núpur, a historic farm with a church that is reached by a sign-posted turning to the left on Road 32 some 4 km beyond Árnes. There is no line of sight from the modern church towards the glaciers, but an excellent view can be gained from the ridge behind, where an earlier chapel might have stood. If not convinced by this, we could imagine a now-forgotten chapel standing somewhere along the spectacular series of basalt and tuff escarpments that line the riverbank on the next stretch of Road 32 proceeding north-east. Enough historic fording places existed on this stretch of the river, with names like Nautavað (a ford suitable for cattle) and Hagavað, to let us imagine our travellers crossing the river without worry, first thing the next morning.

A possible chapel site: the church and crag at Stóri-núpur

Our itinerary is now entering its northward detour, along a route that – short of scaling Hekla – offers the best chance to appreciate the great volcano and its environment. Continuing north-east on Road 32, after crossing the Sandá river our eastward view becomes blocked by the mountain Búrfell on the right and the terrain is marked by ash and lava outcrops. About 20 km from Stóri-núpur, as the road rises over the Búrfell ridge it crosses the Fossá river. Here, there is an option to turn right along a badly rutted track for 2 km, to find a pretty waterfall and picnic site at Hjálparfoss. Just after this turn, a sign on the left points to Stöng, a Viking farm destroyed by Hekla's eruption of 1104, whose well-preserved ruins were excavated in the 20th century. The 6 km track is notoriously bad, and there is an easier way to appreciate Stöng by visiting a full-size replica built at Þjóðveldisbærinn – 'Home of the (early Icelandic) Republic' – in 1974, 1100 years after Iceland's first settlement. To reach it, just after the left turn to Stöng, turn right from Road 32 onto a side-road marked to Búrfellsstöð (a small settlement providing services for the nearby hydroelectric sites), then left to Þjóðveldisbærinn. The replica Viking houses are open from June to August, but you can walk round the outside at any time.

Stöng's best-known chieftain Gaukur, who was suspected of magic skills, left a runic inscription within the Maes Howe tomb on Orkney – a remarkable tie to *King Hereafter*. His message to posterity was *'Þessar rúnar reist sá maðr, er rúnstr er fyrir vestan haf, með þeiri öxi er átti Gaukr Trandilsson fyrir sunnan land'*, which translates as 'These runes were carved by the man most skilled in runes in the western sea, with the axe belonging to Gaukur Þrandilsson from southern lands'.

The church at Skarð

Continuing upstream, Road 32 passes two hydroelectric dams on the Þjórsá and then curves east over a bridge. After 5 or 6 km the road continues as Road F26 which leads to Sprengisandur, another south/north transit route. Here we turn right onto Road 26 which will carry us back southwards to Skarð. The first 26 km of this road have a dirt and gravel surface, with some rockier stretches, and they give a constant close-up view of Hekla and its foothills on the left. After 14 km the Jeep Track F225 ('Landmannaleið') goes off to the left, providing the main approach route for those wanting to climb Hekla (see box). We continue ahead until the road becomes metalled, and then for a further 14 km to Skarð, which we know that Nicholas's team passed on their route between the Þjórsá and Rangá rivers. Five kilometres before Skarð on this road, the farm at Leirubakki offers a hotel and a summer exhibition centre on Hekla (Heklusetrið).

HEKLA

Hekla is far from Iceland's highest mountain but gains majesty from its isolated site, looming above the Þjórsá valley. Different heights are recorded for it, all roughly 1,490 m, as it swells and shrinks at different stages in its eruptive cycle. It lies over a complex of rifts from which lava has emerged in the past both north-east and south-west of Hekla itself, as well as from secondary craters on its flanks. No driveable road comes really close to Hekla and this is partly deliberate, as time would be too short to evacuate traffic at the start of an explosive eruption. For those wishing to ascend the summit, the best-marked approach follows tracks heading southwards, i.e. to the right, from Jeep Track F225 to Landmannalaugar, which runs east from Road 26. The first track reached when coming from Road 26 starts at a point where the mountain Aldan rises to the left of the F225, and another starts by the mountain Valahnúkar a few kilometres further on. These tracks join up to cross the lava-field Skjólkviarhraun and reach the volcano's north-east ridge by Rauðkembingar, then proceed pretty much in a straight line south-west to the highest peak. The ascent can be managed without special mountaineering gear in about 8 hours there and back, but it is a long and not always easy trek, crossing steep and crevassed glacial areas towards the end. It is not recommended outside high

Steam rising from the top of Hekla

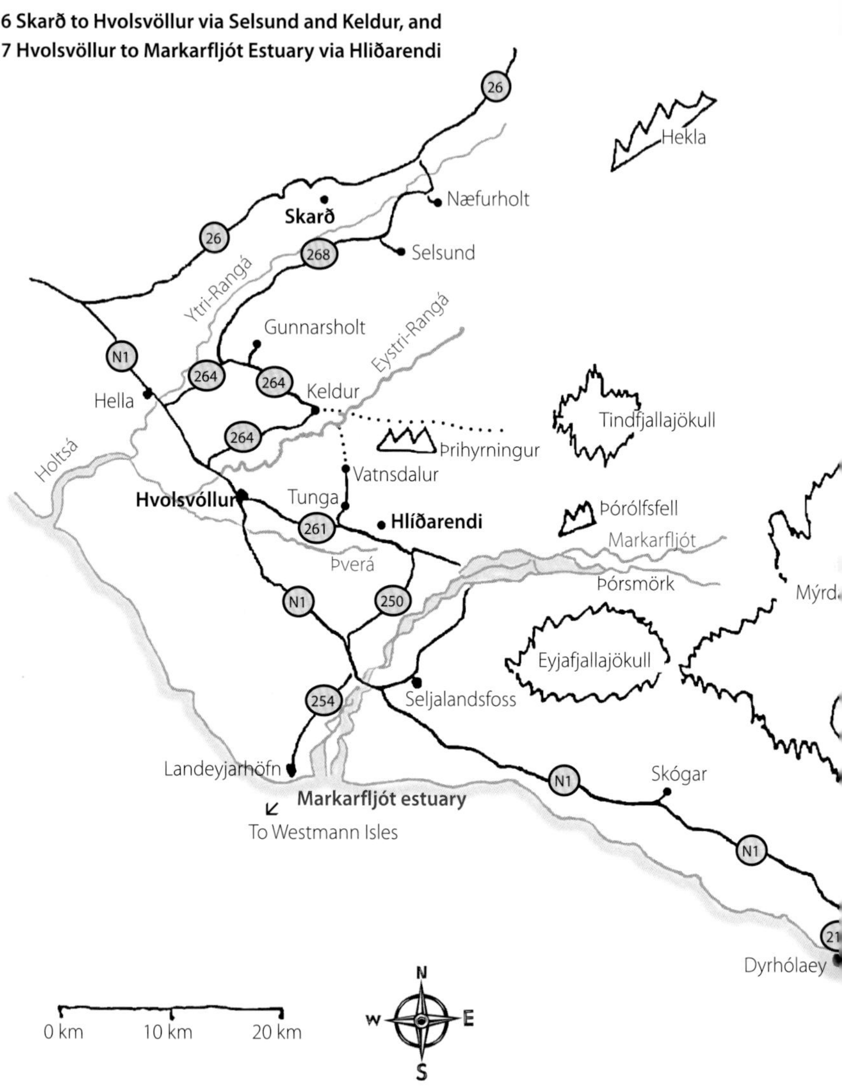

summer, mid-June to August, and even then may become tricky in bad weather and poor visibility. Those attempting it are advised to take reserve clothing and supplies and to consult a local tourist office or guide service. A number of organised hikes are offered. See the Dorothy Dunnett Society website for a list of useful Internet sites.

Skarð

Glímu-Sveinn said 'I do not think we should waste time at Skard. I think we should make straight for Selsund.' (TLWL, *Ch 28)*

Today's Skarð lies off a short, potholed side-road east of Road 26, with an open prospect towards Hekla. The farm used to lie a little further west, but was forced to move by landslides. The small church is particularly charming, set in a churchyard walled with lava blocks. Lava-lined, grass-covered enclosures have also been dug into the mound alongside the farm and some are still in use for storage. A small memorial stone on the mound records thanks from the farm's 20th-century workforce to its owners.

One last theory may be noted here on the possible site of the basalt chapel where Nicholas's party overnighted. Travellers in Iceland during the 18th and 19th century, whose accounts Dorothy Dunnett clearly read, regularly stopped – when heading for Hekla – at a farm with a chapel called Stóruvellir, 6 km south-east from the Nautavað ford on the Þjórsá and 4 km roughly south-west of Skarð. If staying there, the party would have had to make a northward detour to visit Skarð, which might help explain why Glímu-Sveinn advised against it. The old Stóruvellir site is, however, now deserted and not accessible by road, while the modern farm of Stóruvellir is in a different place altogether.

6 Skarð to Hvolsvöllur via Selsund and Keldur

To continue from Skarð to Selsund, where the travellers did stop to rest and eat, we must double back some 10 or 12 km north on Road 26 to a right turn into Road 268 marked to Næfurholt, which together with Selsund is one of the two farms surviving closest to Hekla. The 268 is a dirt road with a rutted, sometimes pebbly and potholed surface that gets somewhat easier after the first 10 km. Its first stretch compensates for the bumpy ride with interesting scenery, starting with a narrow bridge over the Ytri-Rangá (one of two branches of the Rangá, which was the major obstacle the travellers discussed in the chapel) and a rare patch of woodland. Next it runs past eroded lava formations that include examples of pahoehoe lava surfaces, marked in concentric arcs like coiled rope. A tall mountain ridge called Bjólfell (448 m) looms steadily larger on the left, and shortly beyond it, 9 km from the start of Road 268, comes the left turn to Selsund that takes you along a badly rutted road for a couple of kilometres.

Selsund

Selsund itself lies under a mossy lava escarpment, with the white peak of Hekla floating above and the rest of the view closed in by foothills. In 1750, Eggert Ólafsson and Bjarni Pálsson started their inaugural ascent of the volcano here. Today the neat pastures, lively streams and a grove of trees give it an oasis quality and one old turf-roofed building has been preserved, helping to imagine the scene in Nicholas's time.

*Selsund, when they reached it, was deserted. [They] built a fire, and found a pot in which to simmer a snow-broth ... (*TLWL, *Ch 28)*

Bjólfell, in the volcanic desert near Selsund

Return to Road 268 and turn left to continue southwards. The Ytri-Rangá river is intermittently visible on the right and on the left the land is visibly damaged by ash-falls as also described in *To Lie With Lions*. After about 10 km at the farm Kaldbakur on the right, there are protected ruins at a former local assembly site called Þingskálar.

After another 5 km or so, the road becomes metalled for its final stretch beyond the farm Heiði and makes a T-junction with Road 264. Turn left following signs for Keldur. The road passes a site called Gunnarsholt where an agro-technical centre has been established to test ways of reclaiming volcano-damaged land. From here the surface returns to dirt and gravel again, quite driveable but with occasional potholes. Just after the Jeep Track F210 branches off to the left, and as Road 264 bears right towards Hvolsvöllur, driving straight ahead on a short heavily gravelled track will bring us to the folk-museum site of Keldur.

Keldur

Keldur is not named in *To Lie With Lions*, but Nicholas's group must have passed near it to cross the Eystri-Rangá, the second branch of the Rangá, on their final leg to Hlíðarendi, and the site is too interesting to miss. The visitors' parking place is on the right 100 m before the farm. A short walk brings us to a point where several streams of spring-water flow out of the ground and merge, having filtered down through lava-fields above and giving the place its name (*kelda* is one of several Icelandic words for 'spring'). Above on the right lie a church and a long row of turfed buildings, linked by a sunken stone path. There are fine views especially to the mountain Þríhyrningur ('Three-horned') that dominates the plateau of Fljótshlíð ('the slopes above [Markar]fljót') ahead. In fact, Þríhyrningur can appear to have anything from two to seven peaks depending on the angle of sight.

Travelling cross-country as they did, Nicholas's group would have seen the Þríhyrningur mountain as their last obstacle before Hlíðarendi and would have had to find a pass over the plateau west or east of it. At this stage, Paúel Benecke has tried to kill Nicholas and, rescuing Kathi from the river they were trying to cross, Glímu-Sveinn has suffered a heart attack. Benecke is to be left behind and Nicholas and Kathi are to continue south with the sick man tied to his horse. Relying on a primitive map, Nicholas has

to distinguish the mountains of Thríhyrningur and Thórólfsfell and look out for the

Keldur church and Mount Þríhyrningur

canyon of Bleiksárgljúfur; to make the appalling journey alone in the failing light that would take them at least to Hlídarendi. (TLWL, *Ch 29)*

The mention of Þórólfsfell and Bleiksárgljúfur (a gorge on the Bleiksá river) is a little puzzling as these two places lie far to the east, beyond any rational route either to Hlíðarendi or Markarfljót. Perhaps the point was precisely to recognise Þríhyrningur and stay close to it.

At any rate, there is a jeep track today that follows one credible route west of Þríhyrningur. This was the regular track down to the coast for travellers coming from eastern Iceland 'behind the mountains' (i.e. travelling north of Mýrdalsjökull to minimise tricky river crossings). Unfortunately, the northerly part of this route through Engidalur is marked as 'unadopted' by the public authorities and in poor condition, and this author must confess to not having tried it. For those bolder or with better vehicles, it is reached by taking the left turn from Road 264 on to F210 ('Fjallabak syðri') just before Keldur – see above – and then a right turn to Reynifell and Vatnsdalur. The southern part of the track below Vatnsdalur is more easily driveable and is included in the next section of the itinerary.

To finish this section, continue from Keldur for a further 8 km southwards on Road 264 to reach Road N1. At the junction turn left, reaching Hvolsvöllur after 5 km.

Hvolsvöllur

The compact small town of Hvolsvöllur is our gateway to the final stage, as Road 261 – signposted to Fljótshlíð – branches off to the left from Road 1 here to run east towards Hlíðarendi. Just after turning on to Road 261 you will pass Hotel Hvolsvöllur on the left and the Saga Museum, Sögusetrið, on the right. The latter is an ambitious complex dedicated mainly to depicting *Njál's Saga* (see box, over) against its historical background, but including an exhibition on the local cooperative movement (including a re-created shop), a model of Þingvellir in the saga age, a café designed like a Viking drinking-hall, and a shop with useful publications and maps.

Medieval homes at Keldur

NJÁL IN A NUTSHELL AND GUNNAR'S FATE

Njál's Saga vies with *Egil's Saga* for the title of Iceland's greatest, and still arouses strong partisan feelings among Icelanders. Written in the late 13th century but covering events two centuries before, its long text centres upon the love-hate relationship between two households: those of the beardless but wise Njál at Bergþórshvoll on the sea-plains west of the Markarfljót, and Gunnar the good-natured athlete at Hlíðarendi on the Fljótshlíð ridge to the north. Njál and Gunnar were firm friends but their wives Bergþóra and Hallgerður 'Longlegs' started a vendetta, with tit-for-tat killings of servants and minor kinsmen. Eventually the murder of a man called Þórgeir led to Gunnar's being outlawed at the Alþingi and ordered into exile on pain of death. At the last minute Gunnar decided not to go abroad, opening the way for his enemies to come and kill him, which they did with great difficulty only after his wife had refused to let him mend his broken bowstring with her hair, and the attackers had winched off the high timber roof of his hall. Njál's sons, led by the turbulent Skarphéðinn, helped Gunnar's heirs to avenge him.

Later, being misled by the scheming Mörður, Njál´s sons killed their amiable foster-brother Höskuldur, and Höskuldur's most powerful relative Flosi from Svínafell was goaded into leading a party to revenge him. Fearing the fighting prowess of Njál's family, Flosi's band set fire to his home, Bergþórshvoll – considered a cowardly outrage at the time – and all within perished except Kari Sölmundarson, a Viking from the Hebrides who had served with Earl Sigurd the Great of Orkney, Thorfinn's father. Kari survived by breaking out of the half-burned gable end and escaped with his hair on fire. Ultimately, he ended the feud by making terms with Flosi – depicted as a noble and thoughtful character – and marrying into his family. In a strange coincidence, *Orkneyinga Saga* describes Thorfinn as rescuing himself and his wife Groa from the fire set by Rognvald at Orphir in exactly the same way as Kari's escape from Bergþórsvoll, and Dorothy Dunnett narrates the incident in *King Hereafter* (Pt 2, Ch 11).

Those wishing to get closer to Njál's story today can visit modern Bergþórshvoll, where there is still a farm and also a parsonage, by taking Road 255 southwards from Road N1 some 3 km east of Hvolsvöllur and turning left by the coast onto Road 252, from which a short track leads to the site after 6 to 7 km. Archaeological evidence of an early 11th-century fire has been found here, corresponding to the saga date of 1101. As noted above, there is also a good museum display about Njál's epoch at the Saga Museum in Hvolsvöllur.

7 Hvolsvöllur to Markarfljót Estuary via Hlíðarendi

Leave the town on Road 261 and after a few kilometres, around the farm Núpur, you may for the first time on this itinerary see the Mýrdalsjökull ice-cap appearing ahead at the far end of Þórsmörk valley. The section visible here is flat-topped and the crater of Katla lies further south, hidden by the mass of Eyjafjallajökull. After 8 km look for a sign on the left to Tumastaðir, Tunga and Vatnsdalur and turn up this track which shortly degenerates into a rough gravel surface. The farm of Tumastaðir has been a forestry preserve since 1955, and is set among fir and birch woods of rare stature for Iceland. After passing Tunga on the right, look out for a small waterfall stained red with iron deposits – Klittnafoss – on the left, where there is a sign documenting the area's connection with *Njál's Saga*. This was in fact the route taken by Flosi Þórðarson of Svínafell and his allies, who burned Njál's family in their home down on the plain below. They arrived this way 'behind the mountains' from the east, and when escaping after the deed they took cover in a valley within the Þríhyrningur massif. As the road reaches Vatnsdalur, the white peak of Hekla comes into view again and we join the jeep track coming down Engidalur from Keldur (above). Driving back down to Road 261, you may for the first time in a long while actually be following in Nicholas's steps.

Back on Road 261, continue eastwards another 7 to 8 km to arrive at Hlíðarendi, home of the most heroic character in *Njál's Saga*, Gunnar Hámundarson.

Hlíðarendi

Shortly before the travellers have to start relying on his divining to find their way, Kathi reassures Glímu-Sveinn that Nicholas's 'magic' is benign and the Icelander responds

> *... perhaps he is more like Gunnar Hamundarson ... A fine man. His home was in Hlidarendi, where we are going. They say he sits there today, chanting inside his burial mound. (*TLWL, *Ch 29)*

After Gunnar's downfall (explained in the box), the farm of Hlíðarendi remained an important centre with its own church. It would have been a true haven for Nicholas's party, signalling their return to flat and easy terrain. Today, however, the farm site is just a green field, with only the (lately re-built) church to see. It is reached by a short dirt track leading up on the left from Road 261, and you need to keep bearing right to reach the car park by the church. Information boards tell about the earlier settlement and include a plan of how Gunnar's hall may have been constructed. His grave-mound was somewhere nearby, and the saga relates that his son Högni and Njál's son Skarphéðinn had a vision of him there singing a skaldic verse, 'cheerful and with a very happy expression' ('*kátlegur og með gléðibragði miklu*').

In placing such emphasis on Hlíðarendi, could Dorothy Dunnett have been aware of the following? The deserted site of a former tenant farm east of Hlíðarendi church, and reached by a short grassy walk from there, is called Nikulásarhús: literally 'Nicholas's house'. While the buildings were pulled down in 1998, the name is familiar to Icelanders because a respected woman artist, Jónína Sæmundsdóttir (or Nína Sæmundsson as she was known abroad), was born there in 1892. A grove of trees was recently planted on the site in her memory, framing her sculpture *Young Mother*.

For the last leg from Hlíðarendi, we continue on Road 261 up to the junction with

Road 250 marked Vík, which comes just before the farm of Múlakot. Turn right here onto a stony, bumpy road that runs south for 20 km to join Road 1. The poor surface is somewhat offset by an abundance of bird-life in the surrounding gravel and marshy areas. If you stop about halfway you can re-enact one of the most famous scenes in *Njál's Saga*. Heading to the coast to begin his exile, Gunnar of Hlíðarendi slipped to the ground when his horse stumbled, and looking back at his home in Fljótshlíð he spoke:

> *'Fair is the slope [hlíð], so fair that it has never seemed to me so fair: the corn fields are white to harvest, and the home field is mown; and now I will ride back home, and not fare abroad at all.' (Adapted from GW Dasent's translation of 1861)*

Looking back the same way in summer, you may be lucky enough to see the same patches of gold and green on the hillside.

Further along, Road 250 passes on the left a picturesque small mountain called Stóri Dímon, a good place to stop for picnicking, photos or scrambling about. When you reach Road N1, turn left.

After 2 km you can turn right onto Road 254 to Landeyjarhöfn to reach the coast and views of the Westmann Isles, or continue on Road 1 to cross the Markarfljót itself just a little further along and to visit Robin's waterfall (see below). Here our exhausted heroes from *To Lie With Lions* took refuge on their ship, and here the land itinerary ends.

Markarfljót Estuary and Around

The Markarfljót is Iceland's twelfth longest river, just 100 km in length. Its name means 'flowing through meadows', as it rises in the broad valley of Þórsmörk – 'meadows of Thor' – that stretches round the back of the Eyjafjallajökull massif towards Mýrdalsjökull. Fed by melt-waters, the river has a 'braided' structure with constantly shifting channels separated by gravel banks. Today, defensive earthworks hold it within its easternmost bed, but in historic times it ranged over the whole plain below Fljótshlíð and flowed to the sea in at least three more places. The shape of its estuary has also shifted and the outwash sands now reach much further south than in Nicholas's time, so the *Svipa* could have stood in closer to the coast than any modern ship. This is also implied by the fact that Robin could climb a cliff very close to the anchorage:

Robin's look-out place? The falls at Seljalandsfoss

> *He climbed this cliff every day, frequently soaked by the waterfall which flowed over it. The cliff was part of the long range of mountains which formed the base of the Eyjafalla glacier, and the waterfall was the meter by which the*

fishermen of the Markarfljót measured the wind. If the waterfall climbed into the air, they didn't go out. (TLWL, *Ch 28)*

Everything points to this site being the modern beauty spot of Seljalandsfoss. To get there, immediately after crossing the river eastbound on Road N1, turn left onto Road 249 (signposted to Þórsmörk) along the east bank of the river for less than a kilometre. There is a useful set of information boards at the junction of Roads 1 and 249.

Road 254, built in the mid-2000s, runs south from Road N1 along the river's west bank to the new ferry port of Landeyjarhöfn. From here you can get the best possible view of Heimaey and the other Westmann Isles, short of actually going there. Looking west along the coast from the ferry terminal – where a sinister notice warns that parked vehicles may be damaged by sandstorms – a landscape with partially grassed dunes and rocky outcrops amongst the gravel helps to visualise the raised shore where the 15th-century fishermen set up their camps.

Other Sites Mentioned in *To Lie With Lions*

8 Dyrhólaey, Horn and Papey

Whilst Nicholas sailed straight for the Westmann Isles, the Vatachino vessel *Unicorn* took a more northerly course and made first contact with Iceland's east coast. Her commander Martin is described as calling onshore near Papey, at Horn and Dyrhólaey, but without finding any fish of value.

... near the island of Papey ... there was hardly any [fish] to be had ... but [he bartered] for what there was ... three fish ... fifteen fish ... They bought and moved on. ... They got even less stockfish at Horn, and plunged along the black and grey shores to Dyrhólaey, a nightmarish outcrop of rock with two holes in it ... and all they got was a Gothic halibut ... (TLWL, *Ch 23)*

The three locations will be described here in reverse order, as you would come to them if continuing east from the Markarfljót area. Your route from Markarfljót to Dyrhólaey along Road N1 passes other interesting sights including Skógar (literally 'woods'), some 30 km east of Markarfljót: best known for the mighty waterfall Skógafoss, where one may walk behind the waters and scramble up the cliffs to watch from above. Skógar also has an Edda school/hotel, other amenities, and a large museum centre including a 'folk museum' of preserved and re-located historic buildings from the turf-roof era to the 20th century. This is where the trail starts to Fimmvörðuhals, an ice-free mountain saddle between Eyjafjallajökull and Mýrdalsjökull and the first site of the 2010 volcanic outbreak. Between Dyrhólaey and Höfn lies another of Iceland's most-visited sites, the 'iceberg lake' of Jökulsárlón.

Dyrhólaey

'The island with a door-hole' is a rocky promontory 54 km east of Markarfljót. It lies some 180 km along Road N1 from Reykjavík and about 17 km before you reach the town of Vík (see map 6/7).

Take Road 218 (unsurfaced) to the right off Road N1, signposted Dyrhólaey. This will lead you past a couple of farms and over a causeway between wetland areas to the rocky end of the promontory. Here you can turn right to reach a parking place at the top of the cliffs, or carry on to one lower-placed at the end of the outcrop. Both give access to excellent cliff walks. As of the time of writing, the road surfaces once past the farm of Landsalir get pretty bad and the branch road to the top of the cliff is particularly testing.

Named for the natural arch in one of its cliffs, Dyrhólaey is a magnet for visitors because of its huge seabird population, including an estimated 1 million puffins. It is closed in late June to let the nestlings hatch. It forms part of a unique and beautiful landscape complex, with a broad black-sand spit curving eastward from its cliffs. To the east across the bay, the long rocky mountain of Reynisfjall juts into the sea with a set of rock needles called Reynisdrangar in the sea at its tip. Looking inland, a clear day gives an excellent view of the Mýrdalsjökull ice-cap with the huge crater of Katla on top. No boat harbour is in use today, but a historical seamen's base is recorded at Dyrhólahöfn, presumably on the coast near the farm called Dyrhólaey. Another old farm at Landsalir gives its name to a famous cave and hiding-place in low cliffs at the landward end of the promontory.

While in the area, it is worth visiting another old farm and possible beaching site at Reynir under Reynisfjall, reached by Road 215 (properly surfaced) which runs south from Road 1 a further 7 to 8 km east from the Dyrhólaey turn-off. At the end of this track one can park and explore the huge sea-cave of Reynishellir, walk on the black sand beach and clamber on picturesque cliffs. It is easy to understand why several Icelandic films set in Viking times have staged dramatic scenes at this location, but the sudden tides and off-shore currents are dangerous and warning notices should be taken seriously.

Back on Road N1, after 280 km we reach the harbour town of Höfn. It is justly famed for its panoramic view of the south coast outlet glaciers and for its lobsters, and has several museums.

The old farm at Horn

Horn

A sea-side farm on the very south-eastern tip of Iceland, Horn lies 16 km beyond Höfn. Continuing eastwards from the town on Road N1, take the dirt road marked 'Stokksnes' to the right just before entering the Almannaskarð tunnel. The old farm of Horn lay some 5 km along this track, on the left in a flat area under the outer peaks of the steep, jagged and colourful Vestrahorn mountains. It

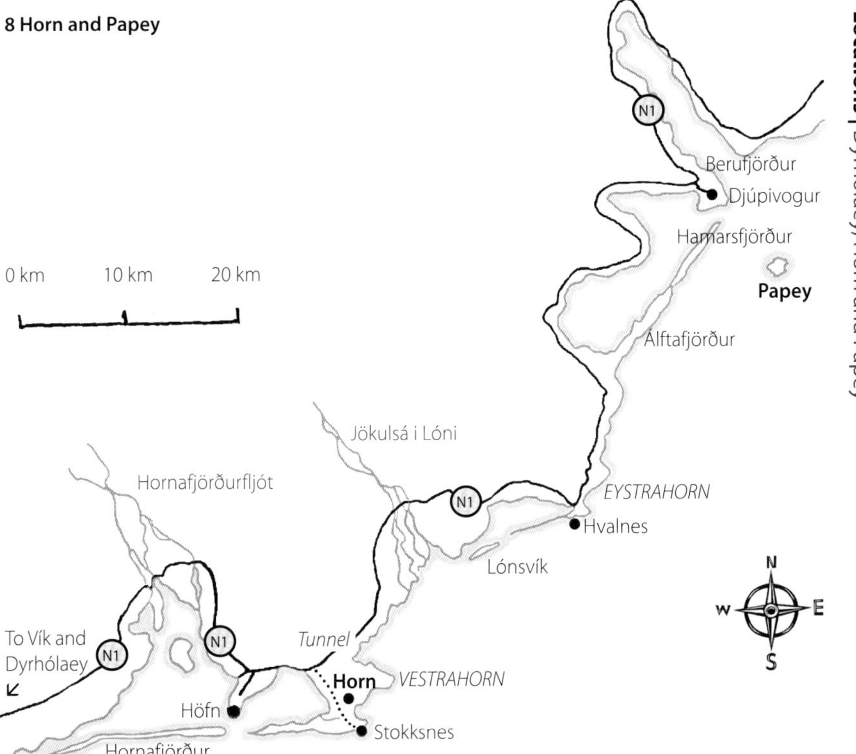

was linked with a fishermen's and seal-hunters' seasonal camp on the sandy promontory further ahead (Stokksnes). In the Cold War, this was the high-security site of a radar station in the NATO air defence network, but can now be explored more freely. Driving right up to the Horn farmhouse site is, however, not allowed because a replica Viking settlement has been built there for use as a film-set.

Proceeding north-eastwards on Road 1, the Almannaskarð tunnel provides a doorway to the eastern coast of Iceland, which is the country's least-visited region but offers many beautiful sights. Papey lies a further 95 km up the coast. At about the halfway point, if you have time in hand, you could stop at Hvalnes on the promontory of Eystrahorn – another ancient farm site with a long sandy spit encircling a salt lagoon, and with superb views. The lagoon hosts hundreds of wild Whooper Swans in summer.

Papey

The island of Papey lies opposite the modern town of Djúpivogur, roughly a third of the way up Iceland's east coast between the inlets of Hamarsfjörður and Berufjörður. Djúpivogur is about 100 km north of Horn. Papey's name means 'priests' island', so it could have been a site of pre-Viking Celtic settlement, and in medieval times it hosted a large farm. This is now deserted but a church and lighthouse remain, and you might be able to arrange a boat trip from Djúpivogur. The surrounding coastal scenery from Eystrahorn up to Neskaupstaður to the north-east is outstandingly beautiful and largely unspoiled.

9 Vestmannaeyjar (Westmann Isles)

The Vestmannaeyjar lie off Iceland's south-west coast opposite the Markarfljót. They are volcanic, created by eruptions from an undersea hot-spot. The latest addition, Surtsey, was created in an eruption lasting from 1963–1967 and is now a nature reserve. Of the eleven sizeable islands, only the largest, Heimaey – 'home island' – is inhabited. The reference to 'men of the West' in the archipelago's name reflects a tale from the time of settlement. Ingólfur Arnarson, the first settler at Reykjavík, found that his brother Hjórleifur had been murdered by his Celtic house-slaves and tracked them down in hiding on the islands, where he killed them all in revenge. Such slaves from Ireland and the Hebrides were 'Westerners' to the Vikings when the latter began raiding from Scandinavia, and the name stuck even when the Iceland settlers themselves had moved further west.

Heimaey had become a first port-of-call and trading place for merchantmen by the 13th century, but was thought a poor place to live – one tribal leader exiled there was mocked for 'chewing on puffins'. In the fish-mad 15th century, just as described in *To Lie With Lions*, it became a popular base both for native and visiting fishermen thanks to the fertility of the surrounding seas and its sheltered deep-water harbour. By 1627 there

9 Vestmannaeyjar (Westmann Isles)

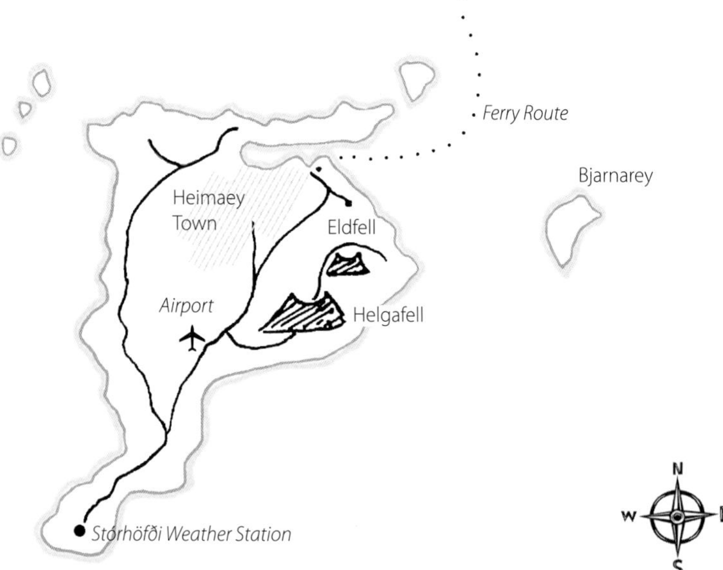

Reynir near Vík, with Katla in the background

was a church and a town of some size on the island: enough to attract three corsair ships from Algiers (locally called 'Turks') who landed there as one of a series of raids in Iceland and carried off 234 inhabitants as slaves. The Lutheran minister, Ólafur Egilsson, was among them, and survived to literally walk home and write his memoirs, now available in English.[3] A strange echo of *Pawn in Frankincense* to discover so far north!

The 1973 eruption that created the new volcano Eldfell was Heimaey's greatest modern adventure. On the night of 23 January, the town's population of over 5,000 was successfully evacuated by sea, leaving a small team behind to rescue further possessions and to try to defend the town against encroaching ash and lava. They could not prevent the destruction of 300 buildings, but an improvised method of spraying the advancing lava with cold water stopped it from flowing to completely block the harbour. In fact, the lava flow extended just far enough to the south and east of the bay to make Heimaey's port safer and more sheltered – meaning, among other things, that today's coastline in this area is quite different from that of Nicholas's time. The inhabitants of Heimaey started moving back in 1974, and rather cheekily set up pipelines to use Eldfell's residual heat for hot-water supply. Some, however, never returned, and the current population is around 4,200.

Today, Heimaey is a settlement with all normal Icelandic amenities, and attractions including the superabundance of birdlife, a nature museum, a modern timber-built church donated from Norway, boat trips (which can include visiting caves where Nicholas's stockfish may have been hidden), mountain and cliff-climbing, and visits to sites connected with the Eldfell eruption. It is also the windiest town in Iceland – lying as it does in the path of all westerly Atlantic storms. The meteorological station on Stórhöfði measured gusts of 52.7 metres per second during a gale in 2009, which is over 180 km (112 miles) per hour and a 40-year (though not necessarily all-time) record. High winds and high seas occasionally also defeat the regular car and passenger ferry services from the mainland, which have traditionally sailed from Þorlákshöfn but now also depart from the new harbour at Landeyjarhöfn on the Markarfljót estuary. Þorlákshöfn lies just off the route described in this guide for reaching the Þjórsá estuary from Reykjavík, and the crossing from there takes 2 hours 45 minutes; Landeyarhöfn is covered in the Hlíðarendi to Markarfljót itinerary and is just 35 minutes from Heimaey by ferry. In some seasons it is also possible to fly to Heimaey from Reykjavík airport, taking around 30 minutes.

As for tracing sites in Heimaey linked to *To Lie With Lions*: it is reasonable to imagine the visiting merchants camping on the same flat, sheltered ground where the modern town lies. The conflict between the *Svipa, Pruss Maiden* and *Unicorn* in chapter 23 takes place just outside the harbour where new land was created by Eldfell, and the *Unicorn* founders at Bót Bay (chapter 25). Fish was traded where the ships waited for Nicholas in the north bay of the harbour (chapter 25). The English ship must have been seen from Helgafell (chapter 28) – the nearest high hill to the town before Eldfell erupted, with a summit that will still give you a view towards the mainland similar to that of the book's characters.

Sites near Reykjavík

Other sites not visited by Nicholas but named in *To Lie With Lions* are the Governor's house at Bessastaðir (chapter 27) and the nearby port of Hafnarfjörður in southwest Iceland where Sersanders had hoped to board the *Unicorn*. The ship arrives there whilst Kathi and Anselm are stranded in Skálholt, and Martin sails for home after picking up

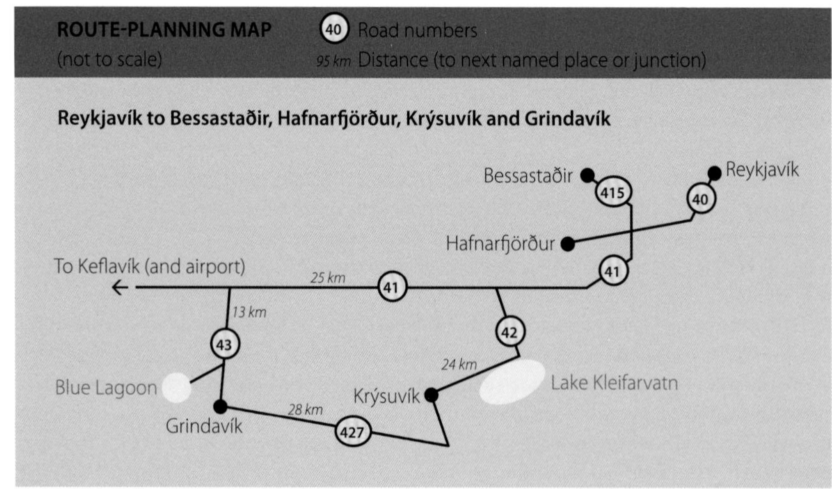

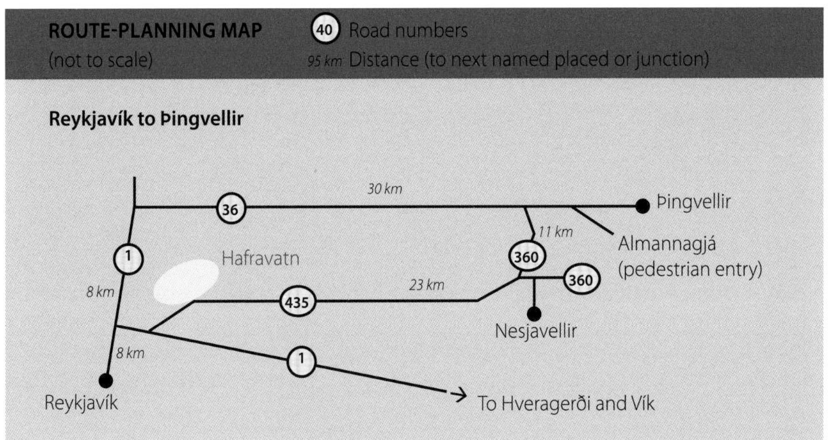

his illicit sulphur mined at Krýsuvík (chapter 26). Before learning what Martin has done, Nicholas speculates that Kathi and her brother might meet the *Unicorn* at the south-coast port of Grindavík instead (chapter 25).

At the former sulphur mines, Krýsuvík

All these places lie near Reykjavík and could be combined in one day's driving. No detailed guide is provided here as the routes are well covered by guide-books (which also describe the visitor attractions). The routes are clearly signed, and generally not challenging – though there is one steep and unsurfaced pass on the way to Krýsuvík. The distance and road chart opposite (not geographically precise or exactly to scale) may help.

Þingvellir

Few visitors to Reykjavík will want to miss visiting the site of Iceland's ancient parliamentary assembly at Þingvellir, which is linked with almost every important turn in the nation's history even if not mentioned in *To Lie With Lions*. A second distance and road chart showing two routes to it is provided above to help those who wish to visit. The assembly site including the 'hill of the law' (Lögberg) is best reaching by taking the turn to Almannagjá, to the right as you come from Reykjavík on Road 36, parking and then walking down the steep-sided fissure. Please note that the alternative route to/from Þingvellir by Roads 1 (South), 435, and 360, which includes very scenic stretches and allows for a visit to the geothermal power plant at Nesjavellir, is closed in winter.

Information and Practical Advice

WEBSITE LINKS

Please visit the Travel Guides page on the website of the Dorothy Dunnett Society, which provides convenient links to all the websites mentioned below, plus additional contacts and information for visitors to Iceland: dunnettcentral.org/travelguides.

Book early – at the time of publishing, Icelandic tourism has been growing at up to 15% a year, and flights and hotels get filled up fast. Christmas is not too early to plan for a trip the following summer.

Museums in the countryside are mostly closed (or only open on request) outside the summer months of May to August. Do make contact beforehand if in any doubt. Reykjavík museums may also be shut on Mondays.

Besides warm clothes and salve for chapped hands, a bright Icelandic day needs sunglasses and sunburn lotion. Insect repellent is useful around wetlands, though the bugs don't bite!

It is unlikely that you will need a visa but you can check on Iceland's official information portal at iceland.is. Further visitor information is available at visiticeland.com.

For travel by car, the best season is mid-May to mid-September, although the rough tracks of the interior may not open until July. Be prepared for weather of any kind at any time: good five-day forecasts (with earthquake and eruption news) are available at the website of the Icelandic Meteorological Office, vedur.is. Wind speeds are especially important to note (a robust Icelandic wind can rip a car door off) but in Iceland they are always expressed in metres per second. The equivalents in miles per hour and km per hour are 1 metre per second = 2.24 miles per hour and 3.6 kilometres per hour.

The Icelandic Road Administration website (vegagerdin.is/english) also carries up-to-date information on road and weather conditions. Road improvements are ongoing and may materially alter both routes and distances – further reason to buy a good road atlas!

All speed limits, bans on off-road driving and safety warnings *should be taken seriously*. The Icelanders tend to be laid-back and laconic about natural dangers, so be extra prudent on a first visit. Quicksands, destructively high winds and dust-storms are hazards not covered by warning signs.

When driving look out for the signs *'Malbik endar'* (a hard-topped road is turning into an unsurfaced one); *'Blindhæð'* (a blind summit or summits); and *'Einbreið brú'* (a bridge only wide enough for one car).

Be sure you know where your next filling station is and also where you can eat next – there are few free-standing restaurants in the countryside, and taking picnic supplies makes sense. In our itinerary area you should never be more than 100 km from a filling station and only those penetrating further into the interior are advised to take spare fuel. The road maps given out by car firms generally have filling stations marked on them and will be more up-to-date than other sources.

IN AN EMERGENCY

All Iceland is one telephone district, so no area-code (or zero) is added before local numbers when calling either from abroad or internally. The international dialling code for Iceland is +354, and depending on the nature of your mobile phone contract, you may or may not have to add it when dialling local numbers from your mobile phone. Mobile phone coverage is complete in our itinerary area and also around the national ring road, except for a small section in the north-east.

The emergency number for police, fire and ambulance services is **112**.

The emergency number of the ICE-SAR volunteer rescue service if you are stranded by a climbing or hiking accident is 570 5900.

The English-language website of the Icelandic Civil Protection authority, Almannavarnir, is a crucial source of information and advice on any major emergency (such as an eruption, earthquake, flood or temporary road closure) that might happen during your visit. It is found at almannavarnir.is, and click on 'English'.

A number to call for car breakdown services will be provided by your car hire company. If using your own car, you may first contact the Icelandic motoring association, FIB, at 511 2112.

Bring the details of your relevant embassy or consulate with you. These can be found on the website of the Icelandic Ministry of Foreign Affairs.

If you are from an EU/EEA country, bring your EHIC card for free emergency medical care.

Bibliography

Ísland sérkort (Hiking Map) no. 2: Gulfoss, Geysir, Hekla.

South Iceland History and Heritage map (Sögukort Íslands series).

Ferðakort Ísland Vegatlas (road atlas) 1:200000, 2012 edition.

Iceland Road Atlas (formerly Iceland Road Guide), Stöng ehf (published annually).

Hjálmar R. Bárðarson, *Hvitá from Source to Sea* (Reykjavík, 1989).

Ari Trausti Guðmundsson, *Living Earth: Outline of the Geology of Iceland*, (Mál og Menning, Reykjavík, 2007).

Örn Sigurðsson, *Sögustaðir Íslands/Historic Sites/Historische Orte* (Mál og Menning, Reykjavík, 2007).

Notes

1 All Icelandic river names quoted in this guide end either with á or with fljót, both of which mean 'river'. At the risk of tautology they are described as 'river' in English, at least on first appearance.
2 See 'An Artist and Her Sources: Dorothy Dunnett's Iceland' by the author, published in *Whispering Gallery* 120, pp. 21–25, for an insight into the various travellers' accounts that may have been used by Dorothy Dunnett when writing about medieval Iceland in *To Lie With Lions*.
3 *The Travels of Reverend Ólafur Egilsson*, ed. Karl Smári Hreinsson and Adam Nichols, Saga Akademia Press, Keflavík, 2011.

Index

U

V

W

Y

Þ

Publishing Information

Published by the Dorothy Dunnett Society,
Edinburgh, Scotland
dorothydunnett.org

First published by the Dorothy Dunnett Society in 2013

Text and Maps: Alyson JK Bailes
Series Editor: Jenny Myers
Editor and Design: Suzanne McNeill

ISBN: 978-0-9570046-2-7

Printed and bound by Printwell Limited,
3 Callon Street, Airdrie, ML6 6BW, Scotland.

Acknowledgements

Many sources and friends have helped in preparing this text. The author wishes especially to thank all concerned at the Dorothy Dunnett Society, and Paul Richardson and Kristmundur Þór Ólafsson in Iceland for their support and expert advice.

The Dorothy Dunnett Society also thanks Penguin Books for permitting us to reproduce the quotations from *To Lie With Lions.*

Photographic and Illustration Credits

Front cover: Hansueli Krapf (Reynir near Vík, with Katla in the background);* Back cover: Alyson Bailes (A possible chapel site: the church and crag at Stóri-núpur); James Cridland (Gullfoss, part-frozen in March);* Text pages: Andreas Tille (17);* Árni Friðriksson (9);* Alyson Bailes (14, 17, 22, 23, 26, 30, 31, 32, 41); Börkur Sigurbjörnsson (27);* Chris (18);* James Cridland (20);* Chris 73 (title page);* Hansueli Krapf (39);* Jóna Þórunn (36);* Rosino (7);* Simone Marchi (34);* Trustees of the British Museum (1, 'View of the Geyser as seen at the commencement of an Eruption', Francis Chesham, 1797).

*These Wikipedia and Wikimedia Commons images are from the named user and are freely available at commons.wikimedia.org under the Creative Commons license.